The Fading Flower

and

Swallow the Sun

TWO PLAYS BY

Mahonri Stewart

© 2012 by Mahonri Stewart

ISBN 978-0-9843603-7-6

Front cover: Kathryn Laycock Little as Emma Smith and Amos Omer as David Hyrum Smith in New Play Project's production of *The Fading Flower*, May–June 2009. Photo by Greg Deakins.

Back cover: Adam Stallard as C.S. Lewis and Tatum Langton as Janie Moore in New Play Project's production of *Swallow the Sun*, May 2008. Photo by Christian Cragun.

All rights reserved.
Printed in the U.S.A.

Published by:
Zarahemla Books
869 East 2680 North
Provo, UT 84604
info@zarahemlabooks.com
ZarahemlaBooks.com

PRAISE FOR THE PLAYS OF MAHONRI STEWART

The Fading Flower

"Stewart is ever the writer of brilliant dialogue. This piece is so powerful and beautifully written it demands competent actors to match the material. These talented and sensitive actors are up to task and are superb.... I am appreciative of Stewart's courage in writing this bold, candid, historically authentic work honoring Emma Hale Smith. The play is an important historical achievement."

— Nan McCulloch, *AML-List*

Swallow the Sun

"An intriguing and compelling production.... The play has a fascination about it that holds the audience's attention.... The story line is wonderful. *Swallow the Sun* is an original play worth seeing."

— Roger Hardy, *Deseret News*

"Stewart is a master writer of rich dialogue, clever and scintillating in the style of Oscar Wilde and George Bernard Shaw. This is a very good play, befitting a fascinating, worthy protagonist in the historical C.S. Lewis."

— Nan McCulloch, *Irreantum*

Farewell to Eden

"I had high expectations, and the play is indeed a powerful and impressive debut. Mahonri Stewart; remember that name.... There's genuine wit and bite in the dialogue, and the characters are sharply drawn."

— Eric Samuelsen, *Irreantum*

"One of the most intelligently written plays I have read in a decade."

— Gary Garrison, Kennedy Center American College Theater Festival Playwriting Chair

"*Farewell to Eden* is brilliant. It's complicated, not very predictable, and has a lot of depth and characterization."

— Sharon Haddock, *Deseret News*

Jinn and Other Myths

"It is cathartic to experience a play like Zion Theatre Company's portrayal of Mahonri Stewart's *Jinn and Other Myths*. This performance does not just entertain, but also challenges you to analyze the artistic material, and also yourself."

— Jocelyn S. Gibbons, Utah Theater Bloggers Association

The Opposing Wheel

"*The Opposing Wheel* is something we don't get on stage very often: high fantasy.... [If you] enjoy fantasy stories like the *Narnia* books, then the show should be irresistible."

— Russel Warne, Utah Theater Bloggers Association

Rings of the Tree

"*Rings of the Tree* has broad appeal. Folks from 8 to 80, especially feminists and young women, will enjoy the play.... The thought-provoking plot twists and turns make the play interesting and keep the audience fully engaged. This is a play you can't leave at the theater; you take it home with you.... I was sincerely moved by [the] play, which left its unique ring around me."

— Nan McCulloch, *AML-List*

"Zion Theatre Company's latest venture, *Rings of the Tree*, is definitely daring—in subject matter, execution, technical effects, and a shocking and potentially controversial resolution.... The plot was interesting, unconventional, unpredictable, and definitely trending right now."

—Paige Guthrie, Utah Theater Bloggers Association

Immortal Hearts and Other Short Plays

"'White Mountain' is...the clear highlight of the first act.... The dialogue seemed natural and easy—it seems Stewart had a handle on the language of the 1800s.... I loved the way dreams played a role in both the theme and the dramatic structure of the play. The verbal retelling of dreams was lovely, but best of all were the staged dreams. They are nicely written and beautifully staged by director Brian Randall....

"['The Death of Eurydice' was the] shining achievement of the evening.... Retellings that bring to light new ideas in ancient stories—with a slightly Mormon twist—are some of my favorite things in the world, and Stewart pulls this off beautifully! I used to think that Stewart was in his element with his historical plays, but I like this piece probably more than I've liked anything else of his that I've read or seen. Not only was the writing solid and interesting, it was accompanied by standout performances by Rachel Baird (who also directed) and Adam Argyle."

—Bianca Morrison Dillard, Utah Theater Bloggers Association

For production rights to *The Fading Flower*, *Swallow the Sun*, or any of
Mahonri Stewart's other plays, contact him directly at mahonristewart@gmail.com.

The Fading Flower

Production History

The Fading Flower first premiered on May 29, 2009, at the Provo Theater by New Play Project. Mahonri Stewart directed the first production, with costume and set design by Anna-Marie Johnson, lighting design by Mandy Lyons, and music provided by Fiddlesticks. The original cast was as follows:

David Hyrum Smith: Amos Omer

Emma Hale Smith: Kathryn Laycock Little

Joseph Smith III: Adam Argyle

Clara Hartshorn: Rachel Baird

Julia Murdock Smith: Jamie Denison

Joseph F. Smith: Alex Barlow

Alexander Smith: Arisael Rivera

Frederick Smith/Amasa Lyman: Adam Stallard

Eliza R. Snow: Heather Jones

Helen Mar Kimball: Sarah-Lucy Hill

Mary Elizabeth Rollins Lightner: Mary Heaps

Brigham Young/Thomas Marsh, Jr.: Brannon Killgo

Joseph Smith, Jr.: Will McCallister

Samuel Smith, Jr./John Taylor/Parley Pratt, Jr.: Brennan Cartwright

Lewis Bidamon/George Q. Cannon: Mahonri Stewart

*Dedicated to
David Hyrum Smith*

*Sweet singer,
Thy faith wasn't mine,
Yet it was*

and

*To my parents,
Who labor for Zion*

But, howsoever thou pursuest this act,
Taint not thy mind, nor let thy soul contrive
Against thy mother aught: leave her to heaven
And to those thorns that in her bosom lodge,
To prick and sting her...

—*Hamlet*, Act I, Scene V

O, what a noble mind is here o'erthrown!...
And I, of ladies most dejected wretched,
That sucked the honey of his music vows,
Now see that noble and sovereign reason,
Like sweet bells jangled, out of tune and harsh;
That unmatched form and feature of blown youth
Blasted with ecstasy...

—*Hamlet*, Act III, Scene I

One woe doth tread upon another's heel,
So fast they follow...

—*Hamlet*, Act IV, Scene I

The Fading Flower

Act One

SCENE ONE

The play begins in the 1860s and spans about two decades in various places in the American Mid-West and West, chiefly Nauvoo, Illinois, and Salt Lake City, Utah. On opposite sides of the stage are two pulpits. The rest of the stage is neutral. Enter JOSEPH SMITH III. *He stands behind the far stage right pulpit.*

JOSEPH III. I come not here of myself, but by the influence of the Spirit. You who call yourselves the Reorganized Church of Jesus Christ of Latter-day Saints have invited me to take a place among you as your leader. I would address a few things first: regarding the much talked about principle of polygamy—I have been told that my father taught such doctrines. I have never believed it, and never can believe it. I believe my father was a good man, and a good man never promulgated such doctrines. Despite what any of you believe about my lineal right to replace my father, I have done so only because the Spirit of God has rested upon me and prompted me in this decision. If the same Spirit which prompts my coming prompts also my reception, I am with you.

(Exit JOSEPH III. *Enter* BRIGHAM YOUNG, *who takes the opposite podium.)*

BRIGHAM. What of Joseph Smith's family? What of the boys? What is Brother Brigham's opinion concerning the matter, you ask me. I have prayed from the beginning for Sister Emma and for the whole family. There is not a man in this Church that has entertained better feelings towards them. Joseph said to me, "God will take care of my children when I am taken." They are in the hands of God, and when they make their appearance before this people, full of His power, there are none but what will say—"Amen! we are ready to receive you."

(Exit BRIGHAM. *Lights raise on* DAVID HYRUM SMITH. *He is a young man in his twenties, with a writing pad and a pencil. He writes thoughtfully. Through sound and light, it is portrayed that* DAVID *is sitting behind a small waterfall. This place is called "David's Chamber." Enter* JULIA SMITH MIDDLETON, *his sister. She is several years his senior.)*

JULIA. I knew you would be here.

DAVID. Julia, you must know that I am not going to forgive you.

JULIA. Aren't you, now?

DAVID. Certainly not. You are a very bad sister.

JULIA. Very bad, indeed.

DAVID. I'm glad that you see my position.

JULIA. Believe me, David, I wish I could I could stay.

DAVID. I'll just have to kidnap you away from that husband of yours.

JULIA. It would serve him right.

DAVID. It's settled, then. Where should we go? Europe? India? China, perhaps?

JULIA. No, no, we'd just go back to the Mansion House. Dress me up as a servant so that John wouldn't recognize me until he was gone.

DAVID. Well, you have to wear a turban, at least.

JULIA. Done. I think a turban is a marvelous disguise. John will think that I'm a mysterious Easterner.

DAVID. From Turkey?

JULIA. From New York.

DAVID. I'm going to miss you terribly, Julia.

JULIA. David—our beloved, our pet of the family.

DAVID. No more talk of pets. I am a man now.

JULIA. I wish you could have stayed a child. I wish we could have kept all of us in that time.

DAVID. I hear that St. Louis is a mighty fine place.

JULIA. Finer than behind this beautiful waterfall of yours? They're calling it David's Chamber now. Where you compose your beautiful poetry.... Do you sing in here?

DAVID. Sometimes.

JULIA. A trapped prince behind sheets of water and all we can hear is his melodious singing. Who should we have save you from your prison? A princess, perhaps? Or a fatherly king?

DAVID. A fatherly king. Our father, come back from the dead to save his son.

JULIA. I'm going to miss your singing.

(JULIA *becomes emotional.*)

DAVID. Julia? I was just joking about—

JULIA. I just want to stay. John... well, he just couldn't stick to anything. Never could stay rooted in one thought, one place.

DAVID. But you'll get to see new places, meet new people—

JULIA. And then there was Elisha! A magician and a tailor! How he could perform that magic! If he could have conjured up a little money now and then, perhaps things would have been better.

DAVID. He certainly made *you* disappear.

JULIA. Not that it protected him from—

DAVID. Julia, why are you—?

JULIA. A bride at 17 and a widow at 22. "Oh, ever thus from childhood's hour, I have seen my fondest hopes decay; I never nursed a tree or flower, but it was the first to fade and die."

DAVID. Is that by Moore?

JULIA. Who am I going to quote poetry to without you or Mother? John indulges me sometimes, but...

DAVID. The wanderer, outward bound.

JULIA. This is a strange world, I think. The longer we live, the more it puzzles me to account for some things.

DAVID. Have some optimism, Julia.

JULIA. I don't think everything is as fine as it looks now. I think in childhood we see everything through a colored glass; it colors everything in most brilliant light and pleases our eye. We grow older and see things through a glass still—but it's a different sort of glass. It's a magnifying one and we see things as they really are.

DAVID. Except that a magnifying glass bring things out of their proportion. You see these griefs as too big.

JULIA. I wish I could take you with me—to cheer me up! Maybe I'll kidnap you.

DAVID. Only if I get to wear the turban.

JULIA. The mysterious Easterner.

DAVID. From New York.

JULIA. I wouldn't have it any other way.

DAVID. St. Louis will be good to you. John will be good to you.

JULIA. I'm going to miss the Fourth of July.

DAVID. I think they celebrate it in St. Louis, too.

JULIA. On the contrary, I'm sure that they don't. Not like here. Do you remember the one in 1855?

DAVID. The one with the elephant.

JULIA. Yes! The elephant and the parades and the games and everything in motion! The fun alive! And—and John kissed me that night.

DAVID. See? See that? Keep that with you. Keep all of those memories with you and let them light your fire in St. Louis.

JULIA. One thing I am glad I won't be here for is this whole "reorganized" business.

DAVID. What do you mean?

JULIA. Well…I'm a Catholic, David.

DAVID. Yes, because you married John. But—

JULIA. *I'm* a Catholic.

DAVID. You're also the daughter of Joseph Smith.

JULIA. Adopted daughter.

DAVID. You've never made the distinction before.

JULIA. I—I didn't mean it like that.

DAVID. Joseph is following in Father's footsteps.

JULIA. And he has my blessing.

DAVID. But not John's.

JULIA. That doesn't matter. Look, David, this issue has caused enough contention with Joe and me. Let's not let religion drive a wedge between us, too.

DAVID. *(Pause)* Agreed.

JULIA. Good. I'm not spending my last day in Nauvoo in theological debates. Now come on, we'll have one last day of fun alive!

DAVID. All right then! Fun alive!

SCENE TWO

The Smith household. Enter EMMA SMITH BIDAMON. EMMA *crosses and sits in a rocking chair, gazing out of a window. Old age is catching up with* EMMA, *as she is time-worn and has known too much pain and disappointment. Enter* JOSEPH SMITH, JUNIOR, *a tall, well-built man in his forties. He's dressed in a suit of pale grays, whites, and other ghostly colors, and is a number of decades older in style than the rest of the characters.* EMMA *continues gazing out the window as she "talks" to* JOSEPH JR., *never looking at him. She fingers a strand of gold beads that hangs about her neck.*

JOSEPH JR. Emma, will you teach my sons to walk in their father's footsteps?

EMMA. Joseph, you're coming back.

JOSEPH JR. Emma, will you teach my sons to walk in their father's footsteps?

EMMA. You're coming back.

JOSEPH JR. Will you teach my sons to walk in their father's footsteps?

EMMA. You're coming back!

JOSEPH JR. Well, if they don't hang me, then I don't know how I'll die.

(JOSEPH JR. *exits. The sounds of a mob and distant guns are heard. Then a man's voice crying, "O Lord my God!"* EMMA *cringes and grips the beads tightly in grief. Enter* FREDERICK SMITH, ALEXANDER SMITH, JOSEPH F. SMITH, *and* SAMUEL H. B. SMITH.)

FREDERICK. Mother—Mother, you have visitors.

(EMMA *doesn't respond; she doesn't hear him.*)

FREDERICK. Mother?

EMMA. Yes, Frederick?

FREDERICK. Mother, do you know these young men?

(EMMA, *for the first time, turns around.*)

EMMA. Joseph?

JOSEPH F. Hello, Aunt Emma.

EMMA. Joseph? As I live, it is Joseph! Why, I would have known you in hell, you look so much like your father.

ALEXANDER. Mother—

EMMA. Oh, yes, where are my manners? I think I've embarrassed you, Alex.

ALEXANDER. Perhaps you shouldn't give possible detractors fuel for the fire?

EMMA. That's enough. So who is this with you, Joseph?

JOSEPH F. Surely you recognize another nephew, Aunt Emma?

SAMUEL. I visited you two years ago. Samuel. Son of your brother-in-law, Samuel.

EMMA. Oh, of course! You've filled out since then.

FREDERICK. We get a lot of visitors here, Samuel. It's hard for Mother to remember them all. Don't be offended.

(Enter JOSEPH SMITH III.)

JOSEPH III. Is it true? Joseph?

JOSEPH F. Joseph?

ALEXANDER. This could get mighty confusing.

(JOSEPH F. and JOSEPH III laugh and shake hands.)

JOSEPH III. You were barely a child when I saw you last!

JOSEPH F. Which would have made you no more than a boy!

EMMA. Oh my.

FREDERICK. Mother?

EMMA. To see you two together—

ALEX. Mother—

EMMA. You both look so like them—and then you, Samuel. Your father didn't survive much longer—

ALEXANDER. Mother, don't disturb yourself by dwelling on morbid thoughts of the past.

JOSEPH F. Excuse me, dear cousin, but your mother may benefit from such reflections.

ALEXANDER. Now don't you try to trap her into your religion, too.

JOSEPH F. That was not the intent of my comment.

EMMA. Boys—

ALEXANDER. Aren't you a missionary now?

FREDERICK. Now Alex, let's not be—

ALEXANDER. Let them answer for themselves, Fred.

JOSEPH F. My purpose is to bring souls unto Christ, Alexander. Whatever motives I have, they are noble ones.

EMMA. Really, boys, please—

ALEXANDER. My family has had enough of posturing Mormon sects trying to bring us into their various versions of the past!

EMMA. Now that is enough!

JOSEPH III. Mother is right, Alex. Joseph may have different religious views than my mother and I, just as you and Frederick have different views from us, but we are still family.

EMMA. Thank you, Joseph.

JOSEPH III. Come, cousins, I'll show you the house.

(Exit JOSEPH III, JOSEPH F., *and* SAMUEL.*)*

ALEXANDER. This group of Briggs' and Gurley's has no more claim to father's legacy than do the Brighamites, whom Joseph F. follows!

FREDERICK. Alex, please, we can talk about this later when we're a little more level-headed.

ALEXANDER. The "Reorganized" Latter-day Saints? What gives them that authority?

EMMA. Well, perhaps they have that authority precisely because they now have Joseph leading them.

ALEXANDER. Joe has become a prophet to a religion looking for a pole to hold them up! Coerced just so that they can tout the name of Joseph Smith again!

EMMA. Show more respect when you speak of your father!

ALEXANDER. *(Pause)* I'm sorry, Mother. But aren't you the one who taught us to avoid these groups?

EMMA. Until you could govern yourselves. You're adults now.

FREDERICK. At least we're supposed to be.

EMMA. Perhaps God is guiding Joseph in this. This group is not like the Brighamites, they're more moderate. They think polygamy and all the other nonsense is just as damnable as we do.

ALEXANDER. Aren't you afraid that it will all start over? We've been safe in Nauvoo because we haven't tried to disturb things—

EMMA. Please, I'm not sure if I can hear—

ALEXANDER. What if the locals find out that they have Mormons in their midst again? Aren't you afraid that the mobs will come back?

EMMA. I'm terrified! I've had death up to my waist, my son, and I am sick of it. But Joseph, like your father, just may be called of God.

ALEXANDER. The Brighamites say the same of Brigham Young and his apostles.

EMMA. God could not condone such practices!

ALEXANDER. Do we pretend to know the mind of God?

(Exit ALEXANDER. EMMA *looks to* FREDERICK, *who comes over and holds his mother by the hand.)*

EMMA. And yet your father claimed to know that very thing.

FREDERICK. The mind of God?

EMMA. He had glimpses, surely, and perhaps even the…the harder doctrines…I thought I had left this behind long ago.

FREDERICK. Or that it had left you. Even thousands of miles away in the wilderness, they haunt you.

EMMA. You've been pretty quiet on the subject.

FREDERICK. I don't pretend to know what God wants. I'm satisfied with the peaceful life you gave us.

THE FADING FLOWER

(FREDERICK *kisses* EMMA *on the cheek and then turns to leave.*)

EMMA. Thank you, Fred.

FREDERICK. I love you, Mama.

EMMA. I've been given the best of families. You're good boys.

(*Exit* FREDERICK.)

SCENE THREE

Enter CLARA HARTSHORN, *a young woman. She kneels and begins to pantomime gardening. Enter* DAVID HYRUM SMITH.

DAVID. Good evening, Miss Hartshorn. A little late to be gardening, isn't it?

CLARA. Oh, Mr. Smith! Well, yes—I'm just finishing up.

DAVID. (*Noting the garden*) Why, clematis and dahliahs! They are my favorite.

CLARA. I know.

DAVID. You do?

CLARA. Yes—we've talked about gardening before, remember?

DAVID. Have we?

CLARA. Well, yes—Oh, never mind that, I—

DAVID. That was at the harvest dance. You have a remarkable memory!

CLARA. (*Nervously going back to her gardening*) Pardon me, Mr. Smith.

DAVID. Pardon you?

CLARA. I'm sorry I—

DAVID. Why—oh.

CLARA. Oh? Oh. No, no, I assure you, Mr. Smith, there is no "oh." Absolutely, positively no "oh."

DAVID. Oh no, let me help you up. You mustn't—

CLARA. But I have dirt on my fingers—

(DAVID *helps* CLARA *up. Startled, neither of them lets go.*)

DAVID. All the better. It looks good upon your hand. I'm not one to shrink away from honest earth, Miss Hartshorn.

CLARA. Clara.

DAVID. Pardon me?

CLARA. Clara. I…like…very much like to be called Clara. That is—oh.

DAVID. Oh.

(CLARA *pulls away, gathering her bonnet, basket, etc.*)

CLARA. Please, please, pardon me. I'm always so—well, I don't know what I am, but truly I'm sorry, Mr. Smith, I—

DAVID. David.

CLARA. Pardon me?

DAVID. I—I very much like to be called David.

CLARA. David.

DAVID. Yes.

CLARA. Goodnight, David.

(*Trying to escape,* CLARA *turns until* DAVID *speaks:*)

DAVID. I like walks.

CLARA. Walks?

DAVID. That's why I'm out, I mean. I like nature and walks and—and was much surprised by such a beautiful flower!

CLARA. Somehow I think you're not talking about the dahlias.

DAVID. I—we've known each other quite a while now, haven't we, Clara?

CLARA. Yes, I suppose so. At a distance.

DAVID. Then it wouldn't be too forward of me to invite you to dinner at my home? They've asked me to sing—you've heard me sing in church, right?

CLARA. Oh, Yes! Well, I mean—

DAVID. Would you like to come?

CLARA. I—well—oh.

DAVID. Oh? If you don't want to—

CLARA. David, that "oh" meant yes.

DAVID. Oh!

CLARA. And what did that "oh" mean?

DAVID. *(With a smile)* That, my lady, is private.

CLARA. Private?

DAVID. Will you take my arm?

CLARA. I—oh dear.

DAVID. We've graduated to oh dear!

CLARA. *(Laughs)* I would love to.

(*Exit* CLARA *and* DAVID.)

SCENE FOUR

It's after dinner at the Smith household. JOSEPH III, EMMA, ALEXANDER, FREDERICK, LEWIS BIDAMON, SAMUEL, *and* CLARA *all listen to* DAVID *and* JOSEPH F. *sing a beautiful harmony from a song written by* DAVID.

DAVID AND JOSEPH F. Then let us be pure as lilies,
    And joyous and glad as the rose,

So when Jesus selecteth his jewels,

In Zion we'll find repose.

Then Praise ye the Lord forever and aye,

For glory and honor are his,

With songs and flowers we'll strew the glad way,

For roses and lilies are his.

EMMA. Bravo, boys.

JOSEPH F. It's an honor to sing for the Elect Lady.

EMMA. It's been a long time since I've been called that.

JOSEPH F. You've been a gracious hostess.

BIDAMON. Don't forget that there are hosts as well as hostesses here.

JOSEPH F. Yes, Mr. Bidamon, you have been very kind to us. Thank you.

BIDAMON. You're just as smooth as oil, aren't you?

JOSEPH F. Pardon me?

EMMA. Now, Major—

BIDAMON. You Mormons are the same whether you live in the East or the West—anything to get more sheep in your fold.

EMMA. Major!

JOSEPH III. Major, we are not here tonight to argue—

BIDAMON. The whole purpose of organized religion: get as many on your side as possible.

JOSEPH III. Major, you know that is not the reason I've made myself a part of this.

ALEXANDER. Some of us don't care about your reasons, Joseph.

BIDAMON. No, he's right, Alex. Follow your heart, my boy, it's your right under the Constitution. But Mormon, Protestant, or Jew, just leave me out of it.

ALEXANDER. None of us can be left out of it now. We've worked for fifteen years to establish our respectability, and now all of that will be dashed to the rocks!

JOSEPH III. Our reputations will hold true.

ALEXANDER. We're already reaping gossip! Especially since you Utah Mormons announced polygamy—

SAMUEL. Would have you preferred us to keep it a secret forever?

ALEXANDER. Are these the examples you want to follow, Brother?

JOSEPH III. We are not the same as the Brighamites!

DAVID. All of you, remember our guests—

ALEXANDER. It's the practices of our guests who are part of those who have made this prejudice against us!

DAVID. Our cousins aren't the only guests here—

CLARA. No, David, it's all right—

JOSEPH III. Yes, let's keep our composure.

ALEXANDER. Composure! Sure, let's pretend that we are all one content, perfect little family.

DAVID. Is this how gentlemen behave, Alexander?

ALEXANDER. I've had enough of this!

 (Exit ALEXANDER.*)*

JOSEPH III. I'll talk to him.

 (Exit JOSEPH III.*)*

FREDERICK. Religion's just gonna divide us all, isn't it? *(To* JOSEPH F. *and* SAMUEL*)* My apologies. I'm just a simple family man with a farm, you see. David, would you and Miss Hartshorn like to walk with me?

DAVID. Clara?

CLARA. Yes. Of course.

 (Exit CLARA, DAVID, *and* FREDERICK.*)*

BIDAMON. What a mess. I'll be off to the tavern for a while, Emma—

EMMA. Major, please, don't go.

BIDAMON. Just a little tonight, Emma, I promise.

(*Exit* BIDAMON. EMMA *sighs.*)

JOSEPH F. Are you all right, Aunt Emma?

EMMA. Oh, boys, boys—

SAMUEL. It's not a simple path anymore, is it?

EMMA. It was never a simple path.

SAMUEL. I suppose not.

EMMA. So, when you're finished with this town, are you off again to do more wandering?

SAMUEL. Wandering? Do you mean missionary work?

EMMA. Yes.

SAMUEL. Of course. I enjoy it.

EMMA. How about you, Joseph?

JOSEPH F. Honestly, I miss home.

EMMA. It will be a splendid day when we all can just stay home with our families.

JOSEPH F. Those of us who still have families.

EMMA. Oh, I'm so thoughtless...

JOSEPH F. I have my sister...and the Church.

EMMA. And you have me. And your cousins.

JOSEPH F. Thank you, Aunt Emma. I appreciate the sentiment.

EMMA. It is important to hold onto what family you have. That's what I see in this new Reorganization, boys: my family. It's almost like the Church revolves around my family now, not my family revolving around the Church.

JOSEPH F. Aunt Emma—

EMMA. You both could be a part of that, you know. Away from the stigma of polygamy and into the arms of your family.

JOSEPH F. Aunt Emma, you know that—

EMMA. Family. Isn't there some loyalty there instead of some religious autocrat in the desert?

SAMUEL. Aunt Emma, please, Brigham Young is a prophet of God, like your husband was—

EMMA. Brigham Young took advantage of my husband's death and stole the reigns of the Church!

JOSEPH F. He was President of the Twelve Apostles. He was given the right by—

EMMA. My boy Joseph was the son of a Prophet. He has that right. You are the sons of my brothers-in-law. There's power in that; people will follow that. Be careful with that power.

JOSEPH F. Are you careful with the power given you?

EMMA. *(Pause)* Let's not bicker. We are family.

JOSEPH F. "Who is my mother? And who are my brethren?... Whosoever shall do the will of my Father which is in heaven, the same is my brother, and sister, and mother."

EMMA. Joseph—

JOSEPH F. When we are among the Saints, then we are among our family.

EMMA. And what of polygamy and all other hellish practices?

JOSEPH F. We're in it for the long haul, Aunt Emma.

EMMA. Well, that's easy for the men to say. Good night, boys.

SAMUEL. Aunt Emma—

EMMA. I said good night.

SAMUEL. Good night.

JOSEPH F. Good night.

(Exit JOSEPH F. *and* SAMUEL. EMMA *clutches at the beads at her neck. Enter* JOSEPH JR.*)*

JOSEPH JR. Emma, will you teach my sons to walk in their father's footsteps?

EMMA. Joseph, you're coming back.

JOSEPH JR. Emma, will you teach my sons to walk in their father's footsteps?

EMMA. You're coming back.

JOSEPH JR. Emma, will you teach my sons to walk in their father's footsteps?

>(EMMA *pauses,* JOSEPH JR. *standing right behind her. There is a moment where* EMMA *almost turns around to actually see* JOSEPH JR., *but then she becomes overcome and exits.* JOSEPH JR. *fades into darkness.*)

SCENE FIVE

> *A Smith household bedroom. Enter* JOSEPH III, JOSEPH F., *and* SAMUEL.

JOSEPH III. I hope you enjoy this room.

SAMUEL. Thank you, Joseph.

JOSEPH III. I believe you'll find the beds comfortable. Be sure to tell me if you have any dreams.

SAMUEL. Dreams?

JOSEPH III. Our cousin John said he had a significant dream in this room. I've had several here as well. I would like you to remember what you dream here tonight and let me know.

JOSEPH F. Certainly.

JOSEPH III. Now, cousins, there is something I would like to ask you.

SAMUEL. Feel free.

JOSEPH III. You know what I have recently accepted—

JOSEPH F. Joseph—

JOSEPH III. I want you to be part of this with me.

SAMUEL. Joseph, we know that you mean well—

JOSEPH F. You haven't the authority to take that place for yourself.

JOSEPH III. My father gave me that authority. When I was a child he—

SAMUEL. We've heard about the infamous blessing Uncle Joseph gave you. And the leadership of the Lord's Church may one day be yours, if you take your place. Brother Brigham has repeatedly—

JOSEPH III. I don't care what that man—

JOSEPH F. Brigham Young said that you are welcome to take your place in Church leadership. But just as with Esau, as with the sons of Israel, that birthright can be lost through apostasy.

JOSEPH III. I am not apostate.

SAMUEL. As we believe we are not.

JOSEPH III. Go no further on your missions. Stop and reflect. No, don't say a word. Reflect and then sleep. Good night.

JOSEPH F. Good night.

SAMUEL. Good night.

   (Exit JOSEPH III.*)*

JOSEPH F. He means to convert us.

SAMUEL. As we mean to convert him.

JOSEPH F. Do we?

SAMUEL. What do you mean?

JOSEPH F. *(Pause)* Let's get some sleep.

SCENE SIX

Enter FREDERICK, DAVID, *and* CLARA.

CLARA. Will you look at those stars tonight! Orion—he's larger than I remember him being,

DAVID. Clara—

CLARA. Yes?

DAVID. I'm sorry for the disturbance in there tonight.

FREDERICK. Our family's in a…transitional period.

CLARA. Your family has been touched by God.

DAVID. When you come away from the squabbling and see those stars, there's such…such…order. Light and order.

CLARA. You have the heart of a poet, David.

FREDERICK. Recite a bit of your poetry to her, David.

DAVID. I only burden my poetry on those with whom I've had a further acquaintance.

CLARA. I am not without my own appreciation of the finer things, sir.

DAVID. Then I hope you don't mind a bit of melancholy.

CLARA. I think that a bit of melancholy would cheer my spirits nicely.

DAVID. My father stood in manhood prime,
At the door of death on the share of time,
The latch was raised by an unseen hand,
And he passed within the better land.
It seems to me that I see his face,
And I sometimes think of his loving ways,
His eyes from pain wore a piteous look,
His Form was bent, his low voice shook,

So I am his poor little fatherless one,

Whose father has passed away.

I must bid him farewell and journey on,

Along life's stormy way.

I wrote it for a little girl who lost her father, but... well...

CLARA. I love it.

DAVID. Thank you for not ridiculing it.

CLARA. You never knew your father, did you?

DAVID. No. His butchery transpired before I was born.

CLARA. Then you are like me, a convert who admires a man they will never know in this life. You do him honor.

FREDERICK. On that we can all agree. He deserved honor.

DAVID. Well, my friend, I am certainly glad you came tonight.

CLARA. Can I truly count you as a friend?

DAVID. You passed the highest standard I put upon anyone; you liked my poetry.

EMMA. *(Off-stage)* David! David, will you come here for a moment?

DAVID. Oh—uh, yes, Mother! I'll be right back, Clara.

FREDERICK. I'll take care of her for you, brother.

(Exit DAVID.*)*

FREDERICK. Not only can David sing and write, but he draws, and paints, and he's a bit of a scientist and naturalist.

CLARA. Yes, David and I have discussed... flowers.

FREDERICK. I do count but one offense against him.

CLARA. It's not possible. He's perfect.

FREDERICK. That he was so ignorant as to not notice that he had your heart long ago.

CLARA. My heart?

FREDERICK. It's obvious—you love him.

CLARA. I—I most certainly do not!

FREDERICK. I'm a married man. I know those feelings when I see them.

CLARA. You think you know the secrets of my heart?

FREDERICK. Well, isn't that why you're upset? Because I guessed it so readily?

CLARA. Mr. Smith, I am not upset!

FREDERICK. Be good to him. Marriage isn't as easy as you suppose.

CLARA. Marriage?!

FREDERICK. Forgive me for being personal, but it…it takes effort. How long have you been acquainted?

CLARA. Since—well, it's been nothing intimate, you understand, but I've been…aware of him for a couple of years, at least.

FREDERICK. My, you have loved him a long time then!

CLARA. I—DO—NOT—LOVE—HIM!

FREDERICK. Don't fret, I'll keep it a secret.

CLARA. Let me repeat myself, Mr. Smith—

FREDERICK. Do you know any man in your acquaintance whom you value more?

CLARA. Of course not, but I—*(She considers this)* Oh my.

FREDERICK. As I said.

CLARA. This is terrible!

FREDERICK. Yes, a very grave situation.

CLARA. No, you don't understand, it's—

FREDERICK. Just remember, act naturally around him. If you don't, then he'll suspect you. Or maybe you want him to suspect you?

(Enter DAVID.)

DAVID. That was peculiar.

FREDERICK. You know how protective Mother gets.

DAVID. What do you mean?

FREDERICK. Nothing. I just believe our little Miss Hartshorn is glad to have her poet back.

CLARA. Fred—

DAVID. Honestly, Fred. They really are nothing more than dabblings.

FREDERICK. He's being humble.

DAVID. No, no, I'm not. It's rather embarrassing, actually. Perhaps I have the poet's heart, but neither his tongue, nor his pen.

CLARA. *(Looks at* FREDERICK, *then gives a resigned, happy smile)* I don't know about that. Let me look at you, David.

DAVID. Ah! I'm being analyzed. Is this a new kind of phrenology?

CLARA. Shush, I need to concentrate. Now stand up straight. Roll those shoulders back; how am I supposed to tell what you are if you hide it with bad posture?

DAVID. I have very good posture!

CLARA. Just roll the shoulders back.

DAVID. As you wish.

CLARA. Hmmm...frmmm... *(Starts humming)* Aha!

DAVID. Aha what? What does "Aha!" mean?

CLARA. I just remembered the title of a song that I've been trying to recall all day.

DAVID. The analysis, the analysis!

CLARA. Patience, David. This is a delicate art.

DAVID. I never fancied you a folk scientist, Clara.

CLARA. From my deductions, you might have the forehead of the poet, but you certainly don't have the nose of the poet.

DAVID. It's more like the nose of the turnip.

CLARA. And your hair... What do you think of his hair, Master Frederick?

FREDERICK. Hmm... The hair of the banker... Perhaps the lawyer.

DAVID. Lawyer! I'll shave off the offending mop!

CLARA. The ears of the politician—

DAVID. Of course, to catch the sound of public opinion.

FREDERICK. I do believe he has the shoulders of the laborer.

CLARA. But the arms of the painter.

DAVID. What is that supposed to mean?

CLARA. It means that I don't expect that you could lift more than a paint brush. Now your hands.... Hmmm.

FREDERICK. I think you may have to inspect them more closely, Clara.

CLARA. Give them to me, David.

DAVID. My hands?

CLARA. I need to get a closer look.

(DAVID *offers* CLARA *his hands and she takes them in her hands, turning them over, inspecting them.*)

DAVID. What's the verdict?

CLARA. *(Looks up and then, startled by his gaze, looks back down)* They're... quite soft.

DAVID. First I have weak arms and then soft hands!

CLARA. No, no, it's not an insult. They are the hands of—

DAVID. Yes?

CLARA. The hands of the gentle romantic.

FREDERICK. *(Catching on)* And his eyes, Clara?

CLARA. His eyes?

FREDERICK. Yes, his eyes.

CLARA. *(Looking back into* DAVID*'s eyes)* His eyes.

FREDERICK. Look deeply. Are they the eyes of the poet?

CLARA. No.

DAVID. No?

CLARA. They're the eyes of the saint.

FREDERICK. And his lips?

DAVID. *(Together:)* My lips?!

CLARA. *(Together:)* His lips?!

FREDERICK. Are you brave enough to investigate his character in that regard?

(*Exit* FREDERICK.)

DAVID. Fred? Fred! Get back here!

CLARA. No. Don't call him back.

(CLARA *gazes at* DAVID, *and grabs his hands again.* DAVID *is startled.*)

CLARA. Shall we continue with our investigation?

DAVID. You mean—

CLARA. Yes.

(*Slowly,* DAVID *places his arms around* CLARA *and* CLARA *places her arms around* DAVID. *Then they go into a kiss. They separate calmly.*)

DAVID. Well?

CLARA. I think I need another analysis.

(*They kiss again, with more energy.*)

SCENE SEVEN

A Smith household bedroom. The lights raise on JOSEPH F. *and* SAMUEL, *packing. Enter* JOSEPH III.

JOSEPH III. Are you preparing to leave so early?

JOSEPH F. We've imposed ourselves too long already.

JOSEPH III. You are no burden.

SAMUEL. We have much work to prepare for.

JOSEPH III. You will have breakfast, at least?

JOSEPH F. Yes, that should be fine.

JOSEPH III. Did you have any dreams?

SAMUEL. No.

JOSEPH III. Truly?

JOSEPH F. I had one.

JOSEPH III. Truly!

JOSEPH F. I'm not sure if you will like it.

JOSEPH III. Let me decide that. You made a promise.

JOSEPH F. I thought I was standing on a large pine raft and was fishing with a hook and line. I pulled out the fish almost as fast as I could bait my hook. I could see into the water at a great depth. Soon I dropped my hook as usual, and no sooner had it sunk below the surface than I saw a huge gar making directly for it. Fearing I would lose my hook, I drew it rapidly out, but the gar was so determined to nab it that he ran out of the water more than half the length of my arm, in vain, endeavoring to snap it. However, I saved my hook and line and carried away my fish.

(JOSEPH III *stands silent at the dream and, somewhat offended, turns to exit.*)

SAMUEL. Joseph?

JOSEPH III. I'll see you at breakfast, gentlemen.

(*Exit* JOSEPH III.)

SAMUEL. You had a dream just like he wanted.

JOSEPH F. Yes a dream, but not just like he wanted; he figured out its meaning. We mustn't ever try to catch that fish, Sam. If he ever stood at the head of those of us at Utah, he would snap all of our lines and lose all of our hooks.

SAMUEL. It's a pity.

JOSEPH F. Are you packed now?

SAMUEL. Yes.

JOSEPH F. Then let's get some breakfast and get out of here.

SCENE EIGHT

EMMA is alone on stage, in a chair, once again clutching her gold beads. JOSEPH JR. enters. He looks about, confused. Again, EMMA never looks at him.

EMMA. Joseph! I thought you had already left to Carthage. Is anything wrong?

JOSEPH JR. Emma, have I forgotten anything?

EMMA. Forgotten?

JOSEPH JR. Do you need anything? Do—do you feel anything?

EMMA. I don't know what you mean, Joseph.

JOSEPH JR. Never mind. (JOSEPH *exits, then re-enters*) I've gone to my horse to leave three times!

EMMA. Joseph?

JOSEPH JR. Emma, the Lord has a blessing to give and he won't let me leave until I give it. (JOSEPH *goes over to* EMMA *and places his hands upon the back of her head, as she continues to sit*) Emma, thou shalt bear a child, and though he should be incarcerated in solid rock, yet he shall come out and make his mark in the world. Call his name David.

(JOSEPH *raises his hands and goes to leave.*)

EMMA. Suppose it be a girl?

JOSEPH. Call him David!

(Exit JOSEPH JR. *Enter* DAVID.*)*

DAVID. Mother—Mother, you sent for me?

EMMA. Yes—yes, I did.

DAVID. Are you all right?

EMMA. Your father prophesied about you, my son.

DAVID. I know.

EMMA. God's servants, there are hard things required of them—and their wives.

DAVID. Yes?

EMMA. Have you thought about marrying?

DAVID. Of course I have.

EMMA. What sort of woman?

DAVID. I...well...

EMMA. Do you care for Clara?

DAVID. I have not informed anyone of such, if I do.

EMMA. You are a prophet's son. You have your pick of the girls within the Church, at least.

DAVID. Clara's within the Church.

EMMA. I just want you to marry well.

DAVID. Mother, you must love Clara, for your boy does, and if you cannot love her, love me enough to make it up. She'll be my wife someday...if all goes well.

EMMA. David, you can't know that.

DAVID. Don't ever tell anybody—if you do, I will be cross.

(Enter JOSEPH III, *distressed.)*

JOSEPH III. Mother!

EMMA. What is it, Joseph? What's wrong?

JOSEPH III. It's Frederick! He was just lying there in his bed, sick, in agony.

EMMA. What?!

DAVID. But where was Anna Maria?

JOSEPH III. From what I could discern of what Fred said, she took little Alice. She's abandoned him.

EMMA. And not telling us that he was sick! Detestable woman!

JOSEPH III. I told him I would come fetch you! You'll know what to do!

EMMA. Of course, of course. David, go get Alexander.

DAVID. Yes, yes, I'll get Alex! Immediately!

(Exit DAVID.)

EMMA. If anything happens to Fred, I'll never forgive that woman.

(Exit EMMA and JOSEPH III.)

SCENE NINE

It is the early hours of the morning. FREDERICK *lies dead with* EMMA *sitting beside his bed in grief, handling her gold beads around her neck.* JOSEPH JR. *enters.*

JOSEPH JR. Emma, will you teach my sons to walk in their father's footsteps?

EMMA. Joseph, please come for me.

JOSEPH JR. Emma, will you—?

EMMA. Joseph, please—I'm so tired.

JOSEPH JR. Emma—

EMMA. Joseph—

(Enter JOSEPH III.)

JOSEPH III. You called for me?

EMMA. *(Startled)* Joseph?

JOSEPH III. Mother, did you call for me?

> *(At this moment,* JOSEPH JR. *brings* FREDERICK *to his feet.* FREDERICK *looks about, marveling at the afterlife, and then squarely looks at his father. He embraces him with an ecstatic, emotional joy.* FREDERICK *and* JOSEPH JR. *exit.)*

EMMA. Oh—no, no, I don't think so.

JOSEPH III. Mother—

EMMA. Joseph, I loved your father. I love him still—

JOSEPH III. I know, Mother.

EMMA. What if I told you that... that he...

JOSEPH III. Told me what?

EMMA. Old griefs plague me at times like these. But your father was a righteous man.

JOSEPH III. I know. There was no blemish on his character, right Mother? We will continue to assert to the world that there was no blemish on his character.

EMMA. He's dead. Like our poor Frederick.

JOSEPH III. You must be tired. Let's get you to bed.

EMMA. I am not tired.

JOSEPH III. Mother, you'll be exhausted—

EMMA. This is my last chance to see my son's face in this world.

JOSEPH. All right, Mother.

> *(Exit* JOSEPH III. EMMA *handles the beads around her neck again. The sounds of the mob,* JOSEPH JR. *crying "O Lord, My God!" and gunshots. Lights dim on* EMMA *and rise on* JOSEPH III, DAVID, *and* ALEXANDER, *sitting separately.)*

ALEXANDER. How much more grief must this family endure? It isn't fair.

JOSEPH III. No, it's not.

ALEXANDER. Joseph?

JOSEPH III. Yes?

ALEXANDER. I—I don't know how to say—

JOSEPH III. What is it?

ALEXANDER. I wish to join your Church.

JOSEPH III. What?

ALEXANDER. I need to know that Fred's still alive somewhere.

JOSEPH III. Then today is a day of joy mingled with sorrow.... Joy mingled with sorrow.

   (Exit JOSEPH III, DAVID, *and* ALEXANDER.*)*

SCENE TEN

Enter BRIGHAM YOUNG *to the stage left pulpit.*

BRIGHAM. One of the Prophet's sons, Alexander Smith, has been among us of late, trying to convert our people. I will speak on this subject for the benefit of a few who are inclined to be giddy-headed, unstable in their ways, and enthusiastic about something they don't understand. The sympathies of the Latter-day Saints are with the family of the martyred prophet. I never saw a day in the world that I would not almost worship that woman, Emma Smith, if she would be a saint instead of being a devil. The Twelve Apostles would have been exceedingly glad if the prophet's family had come with us when we left Nauvoo for the valleys of these mountains. We would have made cradles for them if they had required them, and would have fed them on milk and honey. Emma is naturally a very smart woman—she is subtle and ingenious. She has made her children inherit lies.... Yet there is no good thing I would refuse to do for her if she would only be a righteous woman.

(Exit BRIGHAM YOUNG. *Enter* EMMA *to the stage right pulpit.)*

EMMA. I look upon the case of the Brighamites and the Smith family in Utah as a hard one. May be that God will consider them in their ignorance and convict and convert them, and cleanse them from their abominations, and make them fit for more decent society. I hope he will, that is, those who were taken there when too young to know better.

*(*EMMA *steps away from the pulpit. Enter* JOSEPH III.*)*

EMMA. Is it true?

JOSEPH III. How are you enjoying Plano, Mother?

EMMA. Don't avoid the question. Is it true?

JOSEPH III. Is what true?

EMMA. That you're sending David to Utah.

JOSEPH III. I've nearly made up my mind to do so.

EMMA. You mustn't do it, Joseph.

JOSEPH III. He's been implying and dropping hints, and I can deny him only so much. Alex went—why not him?

EMMA. Deny him to Doomsday. David needs to be protected—

JOSEPH III. He's a man now—

EMMA. He's sensitive—

JOSEPH III. He's a prophet's son. You can't shelter him forever.

EMMA. But why David?

JOSEPH III. David is our most eloquent, our most intelligent, our most diplomatic, our very best missionary. If anyone is going to slay that wild, desert Goliath, it is our David.

EMMA. Joseph—

(Enter DAVID, *unnoticed.)*

JOSEPH III. Mother, do you trust me?

EMMA. It's not about trust.

JOSEPH III. David needs to make his own decisions. If he accepts the call, I intend to announce his and Alex's mission to Utah and California.

DAVID. Are you serious?

EMMA. David, how long have you been there?

DAVID. Is it true?

JOSEPH III. Do you accept the mission?

(DAVID *whoops and embraces* JOSEPH III.)

JOSEPH III. I'll take that as a yes.

DAVID. Yes, yes, yes!

JOSEPH III. It's decided then.

DAVID. Mother, isn't it wonderful?!

EMMA. David—

DAVID. There's only so much a man can take of writing poetry and being Major Bidamon's chore boy without feeling as if his manhood is worthless! Now you will see your son become a man!

EMMA. You've been a blessing to us, David.

DAVID. Now I can make my mark in the world.

EMMA. Just don't be angry at anything they may say about me.

DAVID. Anyone who truly knew you could never say anything horrible about you.

(DAVID *kisses her on the cheek and exits.*)

EMMA. He better come home to me, Joseph.

(*Exit* EMMA, *then* JOSEPH III.)

SCENE ELEVEN

Enter JULIA.

JULIA. Dearest Mother, I wish when you write, you would tell me about the fuss at Salt Lake, for I have never heard a word about it. Your Affectionate Daughter, Julia

(*Exit* JULIA. *Enter* BRIGHAM YOUNG, *sitting at a desk, surrounded by a number of men, including* JOSEPH F., GEORGE Q. CANNON, *and* JOHN TAYLOR.)

BRIGHAM. Brethren, I'm glad you came so quickly. I've had them waiting out there for a while; they may be upset. But I needed you here. I needed them to see the men who knew their father, who knew what he taught us. Those who were with us at Nauvoo—and men like you, John, who mingled your blood with his.

JOHN TAYLOR. We're right behind you, President Young.

BRIGHAM. Let them in, Joseph.

JOSEPH F. Yes, President.

(JOSEPH F. *exits and then returns with* ALEXANDER *and* DAVID. *They are surprised to see so many men.*)

ALEXANDER. What is this? Some sort of conspiracy?

DAVID. Alex—

ALEXANDER. Is this why you left us out there waiting so long, Mr. Young, so you could assemble your den of wolves?

DAVID. Alex—

ALEXANDER. I don't need an editor, David.

BRIGHAM. Boys, if you were only on the right track, I could almost embrace both of you. You do not know how much your father meant to us.

DAVID. We thank you for the sentiment, Governor Young.

ALEXANDER. Yes, that's almost gracious of you.

BRIGHAM. What can I do for you that would take the "almost" out of your statement, Alexander?

ALEXANDER. It is our understanding that you often allow other Churches the use of the Tabernacle on occasion.

BRIGHAM. That is true.

DAVID. That is good of you, sir. We—

ALEXANDER. Would we be allowed to use it, Governor Young?

BRIGHAM. *(Sitting back, studying* ALEXANDER *for a moment)* You've been to Salt Lake before, Alexander. Three years ago? You said some rather unflattering things about me.

ALEXANDER. I report things as I see them, sir.

BRIGHAM. And yet you come to us when you need our help?

ALEXANDER. Do you wish me to say to your face what I think of you?

DAVID. Oh, here we go…

BRIGHAM. Would you be willing to retract the statements from your prior mission?

ALEXANDER. I most certainly would not, sir.

BRIGHAM. You oppose your father's friends very vehemently.

ALEXANDER. If my father were still alive, I really do wonder whether he would still consider you his friends.

BRIGHAM. We are only following the instructions he left us. Why are you so set against us?

ALEXANDER. You've done our family great harm. You've disgraced our father's name, you've disgraced him while you so earnestly give him empty praise, empty adulation.

JOHN TAYLOR. Empty? When other men who you have in your Church's midst abandoned your father because of the principles he taught, we stood firm by him. I still have bullets embedded in my skin from when I was with your father when he died.

DAVID. We know the friendship you showed our father, Elder Taylor.

BRIGHAM. We are often as a people misconstrued and misunderstood. Where did you receive your information? From your mother?

ALEXANDER. Yes, sir, and I have confidence in her words.

GEORGE CANNON. Emma was as strong as stone, as smart as a serpent, boys. She was a grand first lady to your father—but she wouldn't bare up under the principles which we had to carry without her.

ALEXANDER. If you mean polygamy, we understand plenty well your views on that.

BRIGHAM. Has she ever taught you a thing about your father's connection to polygamy? Does she discuss it?

ALEXANDER. We don't infringe upon her in that matter; she doesn't like to discuss it.

JOHN TAYLOR. Don't you see?

ALEXANDER. One thing she has most certainly taught us is that none of you is to be trusted.

BRIGHAM. She is a liar. The damnedest liar that ever lived.

JOHN TAYLOR. President Young, perhaps it's best to...

DAVID. You may as well try to rub silver off of the moon as destroy the purity of my mother's character.

BRIGHAM. She is a powerful woman of influence.

DAVID. You can't diminish her character with your words, sir. Why is it not better to talk of men and principle, and not attack the character of a mother in Israel, whose life is at home, and whose occupation with the care of her family?

JOSEPH F. David, as a mother in Israel, she had the responsibility, the powerful responsibility, to raise you in the truth.

ALEXANDER. And now our mother is attacked by her own family!

JOSEPH F. You weren't thinking so much about family when you attacked my reputation on your last mission, Alexander.

DAVID. Joseph, how can you say such wicked things about our Mother? You've met her, you've partaken of her hospitality.

JOSEPH F. A woman can be mostly good and still have her faults. We all possess our weaknesses. Don't idealize her.

JOHN TAYLOR. Please, let's all calm ourselves. We love you, boys, for your father's sake.

ALEXANDER. That makes no impression upon me. I expect to live long enough to make for myself a name, and the people of God to love me for my own sake.

BRIGHAM. A name, a name, a name. You have not got God enough about you to make a name. You are nothing at all like your father. He was open and frank and outspoken, but you... There is something covered, something hidden, calculated to deceive.

ALEXANDER. Time will tell. I challenge you, Brigham Young, or any other Church representative to a debate.

BRIGHAM. No, I do not care to put your seducing words into this people. They have the Spirit of God; they can tell well enough between light and darkness without you interfering.

ALEXANDER. *(Warming up to an eventual crescendo)* You say you have the truth, what need you fear? You are men in full vigor of mind and reason; we are but boys. If it is as you say, you can easily overcome us if we are in the wrong, but if it proves that we are right, the sooner you get right, the better. Unfortunately for us, a Mormon legislature has made laws prohibiting preaching upon the streets of Utah, so we are denied means used by your missionaries to convert thousands. Yet you have not made it a misdemeanor to preach on the mountainside, and we propose to get the ears of this people!

DAVID. *(Trying to placate)* But we would prefer the Tabernacle. Will you let us use it as you have allowed other faiths?

ALEXANDER. Let's go. It is useless to prolong this controversy.

DAVID. President Young?

BRIGHAM. Boys, I would gladly take you if I did not think it would be taking a viper to my bosom that would sting me to death.

DAVID. Please, sir...

BRIGHAM. *(Pause)* What are your sentiments, Brethren? Shall we allow these boys to use our Tabernacle?

(Each of the men, unanimously, in turn, says, "No.")

BRIGHAM. I'm sorry, David, we don't think it is best to let you have the Tabernacle.

GEORGE CANNON. So far as I'm concerned, I can soon express myself. After we whose hair has grown grey in the service of God, and after we have borne the heat of the day in the persecution and suffering on land and sea, and have labored long and hard in the heat and the cold to build up a name for their father. For these boys to come now and tear down what we have been so many years in building up, to me, is the height of impudence, and I will not give my consent to it.

DAVID. We won't deny that you have traveled far, suffered much and labored hard to build up a name for our father, but what sort of name is it? A name that we his sons are ashamed to meet in good society, and it shall be our life's work to remove from our father's name the stain you have heaped upon it.

JOSEPH F. We are not ashamed of the gospel of Jesus Christ.

ALEXANDER. But we are ashamed of the gospel of Brigham Young.

(Exit DAVID *and* ALEXANDER.*)*

JOHN. It's a pity—their father had such high hopes for them.

SCENE TWELVE

DAVID *has stepped down from preaching and* AMASA LYMAN *comes to him, hand outstretched.*

AMASA. You're a fine speaker, lad.

DAVID. Thank you, sir. And what was your name?

AMASA. Amasa Lyman. I'm one of the Twelve Apostles.

DAVID. Oh. I—I'm glad that you came to hear me speak, sir.

AMASA. I don't blame you for the cool edge in your voice, son.

DAVID. I didn't mean to seem rude.

AMASA. I hear you've had some difficulty with your reception in Salt Lake City. Consider my house a haven of friendship.

DAVID. Uh... thank you. I will gladly oblige that offer, Mr. Lyman.

AMASA. Call me Amasa! Do you have some time? I'll show you some of my favorite places in Salt Lake City.

DAVID. Well, I was hoping we could discuss—

AMASA. We've had enough theology tonight, I think. Now is the time for entertainment. Perhaps we could hike Zion's peak. I know that you're such a naturalist—take your sketch pad!

DAVID. Really, Amasa, as nice as that sounds—

AMASA. I know, of course! The theater!

DAVID. The theater?

AMASA. The Salt Lake Theater is the best playhouse west of the Mississippi—even the professional critics say so.

DAVID. Well, Amasa, don't you think that's a little... base?

AMASA. Base? The theater?

DAVID. Well, that's what my brother says. He says that the theater is historically immoral.

AMASA. You mean that you've never been to the theater?

DAVID. Uhm, no.

AMASA. *(Laughs)* David, you're an absolute novice!

(Enter MARY ELIZABETH LIGHTNER, ELIZA R. SNOW, *and* HELEN MAR WHITNEY, *unnoticed.*)

DAVID. We're not encouraged to take part in such houses of sin.

AMASA. Sin! Your father encouraged theater in Nauvoo. He wept at the production of Pizarro at the Masonic Hall!

DAVID. My father liked the theater?

AMASA. William Law made it a point to bring that very fact up in the *Nauvoo Expositor*. He thought it was a sure sign of corruption in the Prophet! Ha, Ha!

DAVID. Well, if father thought it was all right…

AMASA. There you are! We'll have a fine time tonight, David!

DAVID. Make sure not to tell anyone, will you?

AMASA. Oh, if you're so embarrassed about it, we can even get seats in the balcony. Although, I really don't know whom you'd be hiding from. I think you'll find that we don't have such a puritanical view on the arts here in Utah!

(AMASA *and* DAVID *turn to exit and see the women.*)

MARY ELIZABETH. Good afternoon, David.

DAVID. Good evening, ladies.

ELIZA. Amasa.

AMASA. Good evening, Eliza. Helen. Mary.

ELIZA. It's good to see you. But I hope you've learned to honor the Lord better than when we last talked.

AMASA. Eliza, I'm not sure it's your place to question my—

ELIZA. President Young and your fellow apostles have also questioned it. Séances, spiritualism—not exactly becoming of an apostle of Jesus Christ.

AMASA. I accept the truth wherever I find it. Even in the secret places.

HELEN. The truth. We often don't recognize the truth, even when it's staring us in the face. *(Turns to* DAVID*)* Isn't that right, Mr. Smith?

DAVID. I suppose we can only hope God would reveal it to us, ma'am.

MARY ELIZABETH. *(Studies* DAVID *intently)* What does it matter even if He does, if we aren't ready?

DAVID. *(Uncomfortable, he changes the subject)* What did you think of the speech, ma'am?

MARY ELIZABETH. Interesting views. But I know better.

DAVID. Do you now?

MARY ELIZABETH. David, I've been with this church since its inception. I knew your father since I was a little girl.

DAVID. Excuse me, ma'am, but who did you say you were?

MARY ELIZABETH. You could consider me a kind of relative.

DAVID. A relative?

ELIZA. Mary...

HELEN. Perhaps we should leave.

MARY ELIZABETH. *(With an enigmatic smile)* Good evening, David.

HELEN. Good evening, gentlemen.

ELIZA. And be careful, Elder Lyman.

AMASA. Always the subtle one, Eliza.

   (Exit MARY ELIZABETH, ELIZA, *and* HELEN.*)*

DAVID. Amasa?

AMASA. It's none of my business, getting involved in those kind of affairs, young Master David.

DAVID. But who were they?

AMASA. Eliza Snow, Helen Whitney, and Mary Lightner, women who were very loyal to your father. Stalwarts.

DAVID. But why did they—?

AMASA. Never mind that, never mind that. The theater, the theater!

DAVID. Yes—the theater!

(They both laugh and exit.)

SCENE THIRTEEN

BRIGHAM YOUNG *sits in a desk.* JOSEPH F. *enters.*

JOSEPH F. President Young?

BRIGHAM. Good. You came quickly, Joseph.

JOSEPH F. President Cannon made it sound important.

BRIGHAM. I dare say it is, my boy. It concerns your cousins—

JOSEPH F. They're making quite the fuss.

BRIGHAM. They're your family, Joseph, your blood—

JOSEPH F. The Church and my little sister are the only family I have now. Any other relatives have been nothing but distant foreigners in another land.

BRIGHAM. Joseph, I'm going to ask you to do something very hard.

JOSEPH F. I do not shy away from hard things.

BRIGHAM. Joseph's boys... David is especially eloquent.

JOSEPH F. You have my full support. You know that.

BRIGHAM. We'll need more than your support. We'll need your voice.

JOSEPH F. What do you mean?

BRIGHAM. You're going to give the evidence we need. Get affidavits, get scriptures, get dates, get whatever you can to prove that it was Joseph Smith who received the revelation on polygamy, not me. It will be important that this information comes from you—you are in the best position to tell the truth about your father and Joseph.

JOSEPH F. I will do my best, sir.

BRIGHAM. You've been loyal, Joseph. Both your father and your uncle knew how valuable and rare that quality was.

JOSEPH F. But your knees never faltered, sir.

BRIGHAM. I—I understand their feelings, you know.

JOSEPH F. Whose?

BRIGHAM. Joseph's boys. The Reorganites. Even Emma.

JOSEPH F. Sir?

BRIGHAM. When people fell to the wayside right and left, I just became more convinced that he was a man of God. But polygamy… I saw a man in a coffin and for the first time envied the position of the dead. I told Joseph that it may lead to my apostasy.

JOSEPH F. What did he say to that?

BRIGHAM. He said that God would reveal it to me.

JOSEPH F. And did he?

BRIGHAM. Yes. *(Pause)* But I still find it very annoying that they think I made the damn thing up!

JOSEPH F. President—

BRIGHAM. Joseph said that God would wrench our very heart strings. But we're stronger now. We're loyal.

JOSEPH F. I won't disappoint you. *(Pause)* I've got some research to do, then.

BRIGHAM. Joseph—I hope the Church has been a good family to you.

JOSEPH F. It had some large shoes to fill—but, yes, sir. A very good family.

BRIGHAM. We're not perfect, but we're doing the best we can.

JOSEPH F. I know.

BRIGHAM. Good morning, then.

JOSEPH F. Good morning.

(Exit JOSEPH F. BRIGHAM *stands and goes to a portrait of* JOSEPH JR. JOSEPH JR. *enters.* BRIGHAM *never looks at him, but continues staring at the portrait.* JOSEPH JR. *comes and places his hand on* BRIGHAM's *shoulder. Lights fade to black out.*)

SCENE FOURTEEN

Enter DAVID *onto the stage right podium. He addresses the audience.*

DAVID. They say to me, "My dear young friend, your father taught polygamy and practiced it, and I know it." Well, then in the name of all consistency, why did he in the Times and Seasons, under the date February 1, 1844, just prior to his death, pronounce it a "false and corrupt doctrine," and why did his brother, Hyrum Smith, in the same volume declare that "no such doctrine was taught here, neither is any such thing practiced here?" This was March, 1844, and the summer following, he was killed.

(During this speech, JOSEPH F. *has taken his place on the podium on stage left and now begins his speech, also addressing the audience.)*

JOSEPH F. Many will run after the young Smiths simply because they are the sons of Joseph. These same dizzy-headed people would treat with contempt any other person who preached the same doctrine. In view of this fact, it has been determined to hold a series of meetings in this and other wards, to answer the statements of David Hyrum, and before we are through, we purpose to present testimony to convince any honest mind who hears it, and damn any one who rejects it.

DAVID. Be it remembered that the date of this pretended revelation in favor of polygamy is as early as July 12, 1843, but that it was never published until September, 1852.

JOSEPH F. I have now in my possession and will present the affidavits of twelve women, now living, that they were spiritual wives of Joseph Smith, and so continued to the time of his death. I have the evidences of hundreds of men who had been taught the doctrine of Joseph and Hyrum.

DAVID. In April, 1844, Hyrum Smith made an address to the elders starting on a mission in which he emphatically denied the doctrine and forbade their teaching it.

JOSEPH F. I cannot help the position this places my father and Joseph as to their denials, I only know these facts. But everybody knows the people were not prepared for these things, and it was necessary to be cautious. They were in the midst of enemies, and in a state where this doctrine would have sent them to the penitentiary.

DAVID. They say to me, "Why, my dear young man, his life was in danger, and he was justifiable in telling a lie that he might save it." Christ says: "Break not my commandments for to save your lives."

JOSEPH F. Christ says: "Give not that which is holy unto the dogs, neither cast ye your pearls before the swine, lest they trample them under their feet, and turn again and rend you." He who has ears to hear, let him hear.

DAVID. "Thou shalt not bear false witness."

JOSEPH F. Abraham, Isaac, and Jacob were polygamists. Were they corrupt men?

DAVID. In order to get me to swallow polygamy, you roll up another dose nearly as bad about his lying. Neither will down.

JOSEPH F. Christ, in effect, told His disciples that they should keep secret His Messiahship, that they should keep secret the transfiguration on the mount, that they should keep secret many of His miracles. He told them to hide the truth, until the time was right, so that the Jews wouldn't seek His life before it was His time.

DAVID. Furthermore, my father labored day after day, persecuted, hated, and despised, to bring before men the Book of Mormon—the

Book of Mormon says, "For there shall not any man among you have save it be one wife; and concubines he shall have none."

JOSEPH F. The Book of Mormon says that polygamy is forbidden, except in a certain situation: "If I will, saith the Lord of Hosts, raise up a seed unto me, I will command my people; otherwise they shall hearken unto these things." The Lord has commanded His people. This is the exception written of in that book!

DAVID. See with what consistency they profess to teach me to respect my father, and yet ask me in the next breath to throw aside his valuable, dear-bought, blood-sealed works and testimony for a thing utterly contrary to them in letter, in spirit, that they have given to the world long after he slumbers with the silent dead.

JOSEPH F. Joseph said, "I have constantly said no man shall have but one wife at a time, unless the Lord directs otherwise." There was the hint: the Lord had directed otherwise. The brethren were not free in Nauvoo as they are here; the Devil was raging about Nauvoo, and there were traitors on every hand, men who are now with the Reorganites like William Marks.

DAVID. I am sick, but not of Christ's gospel or sacred books, that I should throw them away for that which is contrary and evil...

JOSEPH F. And when Joseph and Hyrum left Nauvoo, while the mob was after them, and crossed into Iowa, intending to come to the Rocky Mountains and pick out a ridge for the people...

DAVID. But I am sick of seeing this people. Many, many of them go about with that within they dare not declare, fearing for the sake of their bread and butter to speak the convictions of their souls, yielding to the stream of oppression because they dare not stand upon their feet and be men free in the gospel and beneath the flag of our blessed land.

JOSEPH F. It was that man, William Marks, and Emma Smith who joined in writing them a letter, in which they called them cowards. Joseph's great heart was overcome, and he said, "If that is all my best friends care for my life, then I don't care for it," and he and Hyrum came back, gave themselves up, and were taken to Carthage and murdered.

DAVID. O! Saints of God, arise, assert your rights! Be men and women, free and pure; cease to bow submissively to the arm of flesh and the doctrine and commandments of men. Open the word of God and read the doom of evil. Shake the harp of Zion until its harmonies shall drive away the spirit of bondage forever.

JOSEPH F. And the blame rests upon that woman, their mother, Emma Smith. This is hard, but I want these men to know that if they came here to raise their party, we will give them facts, and some of these facts will cut, and if they don't want them told, let them go away and keep their mouths shut. And I say in plain fact, that the blood of Joseph and Hyrum is upon the souls of Marks and Emma Smith, and there it will remain until burned out by the fires of hell!

(*Exit* DAVID *and* JOSEPH F.)

END ACT ONE

Act Two

SCENE ONE

JULIA SMITH, CLARA, *and* DAVID *wait at a train station with luggage for* DAVID. *The sounds of trains, conductors, etc. are heard.*

JULIA. I'm not sure whether this is a good idea.

DAVID. Of course it is.

JULIA. We haven't written much lately. There's been a strain.

DAVID. He's your brother. He used to be your best friend.

JULIA. There's a lot of "used to be" in my life.

DAVID. There he is! Joseph, over here!

JULIA. Here we go.

CLARA. Just breathe.

(*Enter* JOSEPH III.)

JOSEPH III. Julia?

JULIA. Hi, Joe.

JOSEPH III. I wasn't expecting you here.

JULIA. John and I—well, with his...sickness we're back at the Mansion House.

JOSEPH III. Once he learns that alcohol is not medicine, maybe you'll be out of there sooner.

DAVID. Joseph—

JULIA. I wish you and John could get along, Joseph.

JOSEPH III. John has done some very hurtful things, Julia.

JULIA. I know.

JOSEPH III. Trying to turn a man's friends on him because of his religion—

JULIA. John has his...prejudices.

JOSEPH III. Then what a family to marry into!

JULIA. We weren't Mormons then.

DAVID. We've always been Mormons.

JULIA. At that point we were...ambiguous.

DAVID. Well, we're certainly Mormons now.

JULIA. *You're* Mormons now.

CLARA. What we all are is family, John included.

JULIA. Joseph, look at me—

JOSEPH III. My position has changed everything. As much as I don't like what it's done between us—

JULIA. It hasn't done anything. Just a few bumps.

JOSEPH III. I have responsibilities, loyalties—

JULIA. I'm still your little "Jute," aren't I?

JOSEPH III. Is he good to you?

JULIA. My life with John is...complex. But how is that any different than the rest of my life?

JOSEPH III. *(Pause)* It's good to see you.

JULIA. Thank you.

DAVID. *(Breaking the tension)* Well, erm... We have an announcement.

JULIA. An announcement? You don't mean...?

DAVID. Well, we—well, we didn't know when to, but, uhm...

CLARA. We're going to have a baby.

JOSEPH III. A baby? A baby!

(There is laughter and everyone embraces.)

JULIA. *(Like a pair of school girls)* Clara, you and I need to talk.

(JULIA *and* CLARA *go aside, chatting quietly, but enthusiastically.)*

JOSEPH III. You rascal!

DAVID. It's been a bright piece of sunshine in a stressful time.

JOSEPH III. Stressful?

DAVID. Since Alexander and his family have moved in, and Julia, and then the conflicts with Julia's husband, and Pa Bidamon ordering us all around—he's quite upset about the Church not giving us opportunity to work, you know.

JOSEPH III. You and Alexander are needed by the Church.

DAVID. Yet the Church can afford to pay only one of the Smith sons.

JOSEPH III. David, that's not fair.

DAVID. I wasn't criticizing. If God wants us unemployed, we'll be unemployed. Unemployed, but very busy with the Church.

JOSEPH III. You seem tense.

DAVID. I am tense.

JOSEPH III. Always the sensitive one.

DAVID. And Clara, who has all the emotions of a pregnant woman and the inexperience of a newlywed in one.

JOSEPH III. The women need to make sacrifices as well.

DAVID. We men are the amateurs on that subject. She wasn't at all happy that the Church called me to go through the Midwest with you, right as she is in the midst of her pregnancy.

JOSEPH III. But are you happy to go?

DAVID. Overjoyed!

JOSEPH III. Good. Mother, she—she wrote that you've obtained a—a nervous intensity.

DAVID. Does she now?

JOSEPH III. She says that—that you have lost much of your…gentleness.

DAVID. I've just gained confidence, that's all. I'm able to tell people how I feel now.

JOSEPH III. Well, if that's all it is, then. How is your health?

DAVID. The pain near my heart, whatever it is, it's much lighter.

JOSEPH III. Then let's all get some lunch.

DAVID. Lunch would do nicely. *(To* CLARA *and* JULIA.*)* We're getting some lunch.

CLARA. Something lighter, please. My stomach has been—well.

JULIA. We've got to make it easy on the newest Smith.

JOSEPH III. Let me help you with those bags, David.

> (JOSEPH III, CLARA, *and* JULIA *exit.* DAVID *tarries behind for just a moment.)*

DAVID. Once again the wanderer, outward bound.

> *(Exit* DAVID.*)*

SCENE TWO

Enter JOSEPH III. *This time, instead of taking his place at the podium, he sits at a desk that has been placed beside it and begins writing a letter, speaking aloud as he writes:*

JOSEPH III. My dear Uncle William, I have heard of the book you are writing about your career in Mormonism. I have long been engaged in removing from father's memory and from the early church the stigma and blame thrown upon him because of polygamy, and have at last lived to see the cloud rapidly lifting. And I would not consent to see further blame attached by a blunder now. Therefore, Uncle, bear in mind our standing today before the world as defenders of Mormonism, free from polygamy, and go ahead with your reflections. If you are the wise man I think you to be, you will fail to remember anything refuting the lofty standard of character at which we esteem those good men. You can do the cause great good; you can injure it with injudicious sayings.

(Exit JOSEPH III. *Enter* BRIGHAM YOUNG *to the stage left podium.)*

BRIGHAM. I am looking for the time when the Lord will speak to David—he has got to repent of his sins and turn away from iniquity, to cease to do evil and learn to do well. It would be his right to preside over this church, if he would only walk in the path of duty. I hope and pray that he and the whole family will repent and be a holy family. While the sun shines, the water runs, the grass grows, and earth remains, young Joseph Smith will never be the leader of the Latter-day Saints! But David, who was born after the death of his father, I still look to the day to come when the Lord will touch his eyes.

(Exit BRIGHAM YOUNG. *Enter* AMASA LYMAN *and* DAVID.*)*

AMASA. Oh, my dear boy, I had heard that you were in Salt Lake City again! How good it is to see you! Would you care for some cider?

DAVID. No, no, Amasa. I'm fine.

AMASA. Cider, you must at least have some cider! I'd offer you something stronger, but I'm already in enough trouble with the Church as it is—

(AMASA *pours* DAVID *some cider.*)

DAVID. That's why I wanted to come to you, Amasa.

AMASA. Because of my troubled relationship with the Church?

DAVID. I figured you would give me an unbiased view. Being dropped from the Brighamite's quorum of apostles—

AMASA. But not excommunicated!

DAVID. Yes, not excommunicated.

AMASA. Not yet, at least.

DAVID. You were a valuable aid to me and Alexander in the past—well, I was wondering if you could give me the straight truth if I asked you some questions.

AMASA. David?

DAVID. Can you do that for me?

AMASA. Well, of course.

DAVID. I—well, how do I approach this? I have been told that your wife—your plural wife—that Eliza Partridge had been—

AMASA. Married to your father.

DAVID. Yes.

AMASA. You seemed...antagonistic to the idea before.

DAVID. That was before.

AMASA. What changed?

DAVID. I—I insisted that Joseph send me back to Utah. I was becoming so obsessed with the idea of coming back here, making Joseph send me on another mission—he denied me for so long, but finally he relented. I told him that I thought we were letting the very best time pass by us for a raid on Utah.

AMASA. I think you'll find the Brighamites to be as bull-headed as ever.

DAVID. But is there a reason for that bull-headedness? The idea was haunting me—go to Utah, go to Utah—what did God want me here for? To teach, or to be taught? If my brother is right, if my father was never involved with polygamy, then I will preach against the idea until the flesh rots off my bones.

AMASA. But if your brother is wrong?

DAVID. Then they've made a liar out of me.

AMASA. You're entering a complicated world, my boy.

DAVID. Was Eliza Partridge my father's wife before she was yours?

AMASA. Yes.

DAVID. What proof can you give me?

AMASA. Your father taught me the principle himself—

DAVID. What proof can you give me!

AMASA. Calm down, David.

DAVID. Amasa, you don't understand what this is doing to me. I must know this. For the sake of my whole inner world—I must know this!

AMASA. I'll let you to talk to my wife. Then I can make a list of other people. I can give you the names of your father's other wives. Go to them. Talk to them.

DAVID. I don't know what to believe anymore.

AMASA. I understand that feeling very well.

SCENE THREE

HELEN MAR KIMBALL WHITNEY *is reclined in a chair or couch.* ELIZA *enters with a bowl of soup.*

HELEN. Really, Eliza, I'm feeling much—

ELIZA. Hush, my dear.

HELEN. Your administrations and blessings have done wonders.

ELIZA. The Lord helps those who help themselves, Helen. Faith healings work, both you and I know that. But then we are to put our shoulders to the wheel and take the steps to—

HELEN. *(Laughs)* Always ready with a sermon for me, Eliza.

ELIZA. Oh, would you prefer that I leave, then?

HELEN. No. Not for a thousand dollars. Especially since I have an important appointment today, which I want you to be here for.

ELIZA. An appointment?

HELEN. Yes. With someone you once took a keen interest in. I'm certainly glad you've helped me be ready for company. I don't think either of us would want to miss out on this opportunity.

ELIZA. You're being less than forthcoming. Who is this mystery person?

(There is a knock.)

HELEN. And it sounds like our visitor has arrived. *(Calling out)* Horace, my dear, please just send him in.

ELIZA. Well, I must confess, I'm mystified. If you keep this sphinx-like exterior any longer, I'll...

(Enter DAVID. JOSEPH JR. Enters behind him, unseen and ignored by everyone.)

ELIZA. Oh. Oh dear.

DAVID. Mrs. Whitney...and President Young, uh, Snow, uh Prophetess...

ELIZA. I've had many names and titles—don't fret, David.

DAVID. I've seen you speak.

ELIZA. As I've seen you, not to mention all the articles about you in the paper. Helen, what is this about?

HELEN. I'm not sure. It's David here who set up the appointment. Will you have a seat, David?

DAVID. Yes. Thank you. I'm sure that you're confused why I...

ELIZA. You're here to talk about your father. And our relationship to him.

DAVID. Uh, yes. Precisely.

ELIZA. I am good at being precise. And direct.

HELEN. Very direct.

DAVID. Good. I mean...I mean that's what I have come for.

HELEN. Can we get you something to drink, David? Something to calm your nerves?

DAVID. No. No, I'll be fine. I'm just...

ELIZA. So what sort of interview is this to be? President Young told me about your last encounter, and if that's what we can expect, I think I may...

DAVID. No... no, that's not what this is about. I'm not here on behalf of my Church. I'm here for myself.

HELEN. Oh.

ELIZA. Well then, let's get started, shall we?

DAVID. I have heard that you both claim to have been my father's... wives.

ELIZA. We do not merely claim it—it is a fact.

DAVID. Excuse me if this is indelicate, but how do I know that you don't just claim this to.... Again, excuse me, but how do I know that you don't claim this to gain influence?

ELIZA. Gain influence? Are you insinuating—

DAVID. It's a powerful thing in Mormonism to be attached to Joseph Smith. I should know.

ELIZA. Sir, I'm not sure that you understand how offensive such a question is to a—

HELEN. Hold on, Eliza. David, how do much do you know about me?

DAVID. Not much. Just your claims.

HELEN. Can I enlighten you?

DAVID. Go on.

HELEN. I am the daughter of Heber and Vilate Kimball. You have heard of them?

DAVID. Of course. Your father was in the First Presidency when he died. He and your mother were my father's... friends.

HELEN. Two of his most trusted friends.

DAVID. Yes, I know that.

HELEN. Your father taught my father about the principle. My father didn't take it well. He had always been strictly obedient to Joseph...but polygamy hit him hard. Joseph told him to keep it a secret. Even from my mother.

DAVID. That can't be true. My father was honorable. He was honest...

ELIZA. Yes, but he was also a prophet of God. He had to protect God's work. Do you understand what that entails, David?

DAVID. No, not at all. How can God tell someone to do something dishonest?

ELIZA. Dishonest? No, not dishonest. The most honest! A man who understands his priorities is the most honest to his God and the most worthy of...

HELEN. Mm-hm! *(Pause)* I was telling a story.

ELIZA. Excuse me, Helen.

HELEN. Father submitted. But not happily. He wasn't eating, he couldn't sleep.... Mother was very worried. But my father couldn't say a word, you see. So Mother took things into her own hands. She prayed. And God answered. Mother had a vision and God showed her the principle of Celestial Marriage and my father's second wife, Sarah Noon.

DAVID. And she accepted it? Just like that?

ELIZA. Wouldn't you, David, after a vision from Almighty God?

DAVID. How would I know it was from Almighty God?

ELIZA. If you're ignorant of the Gifts of the Spirit, how can you expect to—?

HELEN. Mm-hm!

ELIZA. Sorry.

HELEN. The answer to your question is actually no, David. She accepted it religiously in her mind and in her actions...but her heart was another thing altogether.

ELIZA. Vilate was one of the most staunch in the faith—

HELEN. Yes. At a cost.

(Pause.)

DAVID. Please, go on.

HELEN. The worst came for my mother, and for me, when my Father offered me as a possible wife. You must understand, I was very young.

DAVID. Oh.

HELEN. You must understand, Joseph and I didn't physically live as husband and wife... I was too young. He was still but a distant figure in my future. But through me, my family was sealed to the Prophet. I was the golden link. For this reason alone, I agreed and married him.

DAVID. But... then you didn't... the marriage wasn't...

HELEN. Don't misunderstand. It cost me. Dearly.

DAVID. Wait, in what way did it...?

HELEN. No one except my kind father could have influenced me at the time or brought me to accept a doctrine so utterly repugnant to my former ideas and traditions.

DAVID. Then you doubted? You rebelled?

HELEN. If I had not received it from my dear father's mouth, I should have never received it as God's sacred truth. Eliza, can you take over for a moment? I... I would like to compose myself before I continue.

ELIZA. Of course, Helen.

DAVID. Wait, but—

ELIZA. I have heard that you're known for your sensitivity, David. Make use of that quality now.

DAVID. Yes. Of course. I apologize.

ELIZA. Now, my boy, you also have to understand that to some like Helen, this was a great sacrifice. To me, well, despite the sacrifices, it was one of the greatest blessings of my life.

DAVID. I have a hard time accepting that.

ELIZA. I doubted at first, when I started hearing the rumors. I thought it was...repugnant.

DAVID. And are you sure you weren't wrong?

ELIZA. I came to the conclusion that if this was truly the time where all things were to be restored, it meant ALL things. Even the blessings of Abraham, Isaac, and Jacob. But this was all very intellectual, you see, distant. But when I was actually confronted with the fact that I was going to live it, well, that was different. But as I increased in knowledge of the principle, I grew in love with it, and today I esteem it as a precious, sacred principle.

DAVID. How can you say that? How can any woman say that, seeing how it demeans their sex? No, no, I won't accept that, I can't accept that!

HELEN. David.

DAVID. No, Mrs. Whitney, I won't hear any more of these false—

HELEN. I agreed with you, David. Once.

DAVID. Then it was a mistake for you to succumb to the lusts of wicked men. For women as grand as the both of you to—

HELEN. Wait. Calm yourself.

DAVID. *(Rising to his feet)* Calm? Calm! You tell me that my Father was not the man I thought him to be and you want me to be calm?!

HELEN. Precisely.

(JOSEPH JR. *comes and places his hand on* DAVID's *shoulder. The tension, stress and fear within* DAVID *are immediately placated. There is a significant pause.*)

DAVID. All right.

(JOSEPH JR. *releases his hand from* DAVID *and* DAVID *sits, once again ready to listen.*)

HELEN. Thank you. Even after Joseph's death, I rebelled in my heart. Even after I was re-married to my sweetheart Horace, I resented that

I wasn't truly his and his alone. And when I saw the pains that still tore and ravaged my mother's heart, I steeled my heart against it all. I still went to Winter Quarters when we were driven out of Nauvoo. I remained with the Saints in a front of strength... but still I was depressed... depressed and angry.

DAVID. Good. Good, I say! And I tell you, Mrs. Whitney, if you let those feelings back into your heart and see how you have been misused, then you will find those who are willing to accept you with open arms and bring you back into a righteous society.

HELEN. No!

DAVID. But, Mrs. Whitney, if this has caused you so much torturous pain, why on earth would you—

HELEN. I lost my first child in Winter Quarters... and then my second. I have lost five children in my life. Your mother's not the only one who knows that kind of pain. I wanted to die. I asked God to take me to my... lovely... my lovely, sweet, little ones. I was very sick and I expected to get my death wish. For three months I lay a portion of the time like one dead.... I tasted of the punishment which is prepared for those who reject any of the principles of this Gospel. But... oh, then I learned that plural marriage is a celestial principle. I saw the danger of rebelling against the Lord's anointed.... During that season I lost my speech, forgot the names of everybody and everything, and was living in another sphere. Satan desired to clip my glory, but when that was thwarted he tried every possible way to destroy my tabernacle. The evil spirits caused me to believe that I was worthless, beyond redemption...

DAVID. Satan? You believe that literally or figuratively?

HELEN. Do you not believe in Satan?

DAVID. Theoretically... yes. But what you're saying... evil spirits...

HELEN. *(Pause)* Someday you shall see them, too, David.

DAVID. Pardon me?

HELEN. In fact, you've allowed yourself already to come under their influence, haven't you? I've heard you spend a lot of time with Amasa Lyman these days. Do you...partake of his table?

DAVID. I've decided to seek truth wherever it is—his as much as yours.

HELEN. *(Pause)* I was under the chains of hell, David. I had my last struggle and resolved that the spirits should buffet me no longer. I fasted every day for one week, and every day I gained till I had won the victory. I was just as sensible of the presence of holy spirits around my bedside as I had been of the evil ones. It was one of the happiest days of my life. I immediately called my mother to my bedside. I knew her heart was weighed down in sorrow because of polygamy. I never before spoke with such eloquence, and she knew that it was not myself. She was so affected that she sobbed until I ceased. I assured her that father loved her, but he had a work to do; she must rise above her feelings and seek for the Holy Comforter, and though it rent her heart, she must uphold him, for he had only taken wives in obedience to a holy principle. My strength returned that instant, and I was healed. *(Pause)* You know, Eliza, I'm feeling much better.

DAVID. That's...I'm sure you feel that's inspiring, however...

ELIZA. More howevers?

DAVID. I still can't see how the holy monogamy between one man and one woman, like Adam and Eve, should ever be overthrown for such a wretched principle of oppression?

ELIZA. Oppression?

DAVID. Do you dispute it? I've seen how the women here are often neglected, how their rights are taken from them, how they dwindle in sorrow.

ELIZA. David, where is your wife?

DAVID. What?

ELIZA. Your wife, is she here with you in Utah?

DAVID. No.

ELIZA. Have you left her in comfort?

DAVID. She's with Mother.

ELIZA. And she and your mother have a strong relationship?

DAVID. Not...not precisely.

ELIZA. Supporting her has been your number one object?

DAVID. I...I am busy here.

ELIZA. And this is the glory of monogamy!

DAVID. That is different! I...I am doing this...this...

ELIZA. For the Lord?

DAVID. Yes.

ELIZA. Sounds familiar. And your stepfather, Lewis Bidamon—

DAVID. The Major has nothing to do with—

ELIZA. He's good to your mother?

DAVID. He's as good as any man can be expected—

ELIZA. I heard that he had an affair.

DAVID. That...is true.

ELIZA. And that your mother, bless her heart, took the illegitimate child in and is raising him as her own. And that she has brought in the mistress as her servant so that she can support herself?

DAVID. That is also true. But you don't understand...

ELIZA. And you cast aspersions and insults upon us, and then turn a blind eye to what happens in your own home!

DAVID. But that's not the ideal! That's not how it's supposed to be!

HELEN. Precisely. We know that there are those who practice the principle who abuse it. But Utah women are much more liberated than many monogamous women in the rest of this nation.

DAVID. If you think that excuses...

HELEN. There are more women doctors per capita in Utah than anywhere else in the nation. Our women, instead of being told simply to be reliant, have been urged to become educated and skilled. President Young even once said that he would have no issues with a woman becoming the President of the United States. And you say that WE are the oppressive ones, while your virtuous, monogamous men cheat on their wives and while your own wife languishes in loneliness, poverty, and insecurity?

DAVID. I love Clara.

HELEN. And many of our husbands love us. But whether in polygamy or monogamy, men will be held responsible for how they treat their wives. It is not so much the system one is under, but how it is executed which really counts in the end. Where much is given, much is required.

DAVID. I think I am done here.

ELIZA. David, wait. One more story—

DAVID. No!

ELIZA. Your father...when he died...I was devastated. I wanted to die so that I could go with him. Your father...his spirit came to me.

DAVID. What?

ELIZA. He told me:

JOSEPH JR. My work upon the earth is completed as far as the mortal tabernacle is concerned. But, Eliza, yours is not. The Lord desires you, and so does your husband, to live many years and assist in carrying on the great latter-day work which I was chosen to establish. Have courage, dear Eliza. Others need you to cheer and lighten their burdens. Don't think of your loneliness.... Help others with *their* sorrows.

DAVID. President Snow, sometimes...sometimes we give too much credence to dreams.

ELIZA. This was not a dream.

DAVID. So you say.

ELIZA. David...when you were born...I...I wrote a poem for you.

DAVID. For me?

ELIZA. Even then, we had high hopes for you. May I recite it to you?

DAVID. *(Pause)* Yes.

ELIZA. Sinless as celestial spirits—
Lovely as a morning flow'r
Comes the smiling infant stranger
In an evil-omen'd hour.
In an hour of lamentation—
In a time—a season when
Zion's noblest sons are fallen,
By the hands of wicked men.
In an hour when peace and safety
Have the civil banner fled—
In a day when legal justice
Covers its dishonor'd head
In an age when saints must suffer
Without mercy or redress;
Comes to meet a generation
That has made it fatherless
Not to share a father's fondness—
Not to know its father's worth—
By the arm of persecution
'Tis an orphan at its birth!
Smile, sweet babe! Thou art unconscious
Of thy great, untimely loss!
The broad stroke of thy bereavement,
Zion's pathway seem'd to cross!

Till in childhood thou had'st known him,
Had the age, thy father spar'd;
The endearment of remembrance,
Through thy life time thou had'st shar'd.
Thou may'st draw from love and kindness
All a mother can bestow;
But alas! On earth, a father
You art destin'd not to know!

DAVID. Eliza…Thank you. Especially in the form of a poem… I…thank you.

ELIZA. I…I know people think I'm severe, sometimes even cold. But my heart is tender, David, and it has a very warm place for you.

DAVID. If this principle is wrong, may God cleanse you, for you truly are beautiful women.

ELIZA. And if it's right?

DAVID. Then may God not let it destroy us.

(Exit DAVID.)

SCENE FOUR

Enter CLARA, who is six months pregnant and making bread. Enter EMMA. EMMA notes CLARA with disapproval.

EMMA. No, dear, you're not doing that right.

CLARA. I am doing it right.

EMMA. No, like this—*(Starts interfering)*—that will get the lumps out.

CLARA. I know how to make bread, Mother Smith.

EMMA. And I'm teaching you how to make better bread.

CLARA. I was doing fine.

EMMA. You know, dear, I can take over this if you want to check on the pudding.

CLARA. I was enjoying the bread.

EMMA. But you aren't getting out the lumps.

CLARA. *(Crying)* I know how to make bread!

EMMA. Clara...I'm sorry. Come here.

(EMMA *embraces* CLARA.)

CLARA. I'm sorry. It's a stupid thing to cry about, bread and all—

EMMA. You're not crying about the bread.

CLARA. I'm...It's been hard. I feel all alone.... I miss him.

EMMA. Believe me, I remember that kind of loneliness.

CLARA. I—I didn't mean to—

EMMA. Of course you didn't. We all have our torments, that's all. My dear...I know I'm harsh on you sometimes, but I hope...I hope you know...

CLARA. I think I understand.

EMMA. But you need to hear it. Sometimes we can become possessive of our...loved ones. We just don't want to lose them...to lose their love.

CLARA. I can understand that.

EMMA. You know, my parents didn't approve of my Joseph.... Hm, that's putting it mildly. They...they hated...losing me to him. But Joseph's parents, they accepted me with open arms.

CLARA. You had a good relationship with Mother Smith, then?

EMMA. She was one of my most valiant supporters.

CLARA. Do you think that you can...?

EMMA. I can certainly try. It's just...

CLARA. I'm far from perfect, but I'm trying to deserve David.

EMMA. Clara, it's less about that than...

CLARA. I'm listening.

EMMA. It seems if I let those I love out of my sight, even for a moment, I...I lose them. Yet the harder I hold onto them, the more they push away...

CLARA. David's hard to pin down, I know.

EMMA. Yes, David...and...My dear, I feel in my heart to tell you...oh, it's so hard—

CLARA. Don't you fret. I understand.

EMMA. No, you don't...I—

CLARA. This is causing you undue stress.

EMMA. But—

CLARA. No, you don't need to say it. I understand.

EMMA. No—

CLARA. Merry Christmas, Mother Smith.

EMMA. *(Resigning)* Merry Christmas.

SCENE FIVE

AMASA LYMAN's *home.* AMASA *answers a knock at the door.*

AMASA. I'm coming, I'm coming—Oh. Elder Smith. Come in.
(Enter JOSEPH F.)

JOSEPH F. Is it true, Amasa?

AMASA. Joseph, welcome. Can I get you—

JOSEPH F. Please, Amasa, don't dodge the question.

AMASA. What question would that be, Joseph? Is what true?

JOSEPH F. I have heard reports that you've continued in your séances—

AMASA. If I have, that is my personal—

JOSEPH F. —And that you have dragged my cousin David into the mix.

AMASA. David is an adult and can choose to engage in—

JOSEPH F. It's devilry! You're letting yourself open to being deceived!

AMASA. Come see for yourself and determine whether—

JOSEPH F. No!

AMASA. Well, obviously you'd be a little sensitive about it, but—

JOSEPH F. Sensitive? This goes way beyond sensitive, Amasa. I know that David and I have been pitted against each other but—

AMASA. But you're family.

JOSEPH F. *(Pause)* I don't want to see him caught up in something he can't get out of. I don't know what kind of hellish influences you've allowed to prey on him.

AMASA. I am not a servant of Satan.

JOSEPH F. But perhaps you are his toy.

AMASA. I would appreciate it if you left my home, Elder Smith.

JOSEPH F. It was bad enough to get yourself involved in it, but to drag in poor David... You may think that séances and such give you a sense of power, Amasa, but once you call upon those spirits, who has power over whom?

AMASA. I said leave my home.

JOSEPH F. Be careful, Amasa. Please, be careful.

(Exit JOSEPH F., *then* AMASA.*)*

SCENE SIX

Enter MARY ELIZABETH LIGHTNER. *She sits as if on her porch, doing some needlework. Outdoor sounds such as birds, etc. are heard. Enter* DAVID, *followed once again by* JOSEPH JR.

DAVID. Ma'am? Mary Lightner?

MARY LIGHTNER. *(Not looking up from her work)* Hm? Who is it?

DAVID. I'm Mr. Smith. David Hyrum Smith.

MARY LIGHTNER. *(Looking up, startled)* Joseph's son?

DAVID. Yes, ma'am. That's what I'm told.

MARY. *(Pause, then laughs)* Well, I'll be! Well, I haven't seen you since that one speech you gave—of course you didn't know who I was.

DAVID. I suppose you never expected a visit from me.

MARY. I've never been so surprised in my entire life!

DAVID. I can't say that I ever thought I'd take this trip, either.

MARY. I'd say! Take a seat, my boy.

DAVID. Thank you.

MARY. Bright, sunny day, isn't it?

DAVID. Not to be abrupt, ma'am, but I didn't really come here to talk about that.

MARY. Of course you didn't. I know exactly why you've come here.

DAVID. I suppose you do. I didn't know who you were when you came to hear me speak all that time ago, but I know who you are now.

MARY. And to answer your question, yes, I was one of your father's wives.

DAVID. So I'm told.

MARY. Is that all you've come to hear then?

DAVID. Is that all you have to say?

MARY. I have plenty I could tell, depending on what you want to hear.

DAVID. I want to hear the truth.

MARY. The truth! *(Laughs)* That's a little broad, isn't it? What specific truths?

DAVID. Was my father an adulterer?

MARY. *(Becoming very serious)* Never use that word in connection with your father again.

DAVID. With all due respect, ma'am, with the way I've been brought up—

MARY. Brought up! If your father was a polygamist, then your mother weaned you off lies.

DAVID. My mother is a virtuous woman.

MARY. And your father was a virtuous man. They both can be virtuous, you know, despite their imperfections.

DAVID. What would you know of my mother?

MARY. Quite a bit, actually. I had a long time to watch her. Your father said she thought highly of me.

DAVID. I doubt she would still think as highly.

MARY. If you call him an adulterer, you call me an adulterer.

DAVID. I do not rule that option out.

MARY. I was told you were the diplomatic one.

DAVID. There are a lot of things that I've had to alter lately.

MARY. I believe it. I know this is trying information, my boy, but your father was a true prophet.

DAVID. I used to be sure of that myself.... But how could he be, if he taught something such as...such as...

MARY. The principle was given to him before he gave it to the Church. An angel came to him, and the last time he came with a drawn sword in his hand and told Joseph if he did not go into the principle, he would slay him. Joseph argued with the angel, quoted scripture at him, said it was an abomination.

DAVID. That could be a story, a Brighamite excuse—

MARY. My boy, you think you are so clever, so intelligent. You are ignorant.

DAVID. Ignorant!

MARY. Listen, I had been dreaming for a number of years that I was his wife. I thought I was a great sinner. I prayed to God to take it from me—but then Joseph sent for me and told me of it, explained it. I still didn't believe it.

DAVID. Perhaps you shouldn't have abandoned that belief.

> *(During this upcoming exchange, MARY never looks at JOSEPH JR., but talks to him as if he were right there, both of them looking out to the audience as if they were looking at each other. Then when talking to DAVID, she switches back to him. This back and forth plays throughout the rest of the scene.)*

MARY. I told him, "Don't you think it was an angel of the devil that told you of these things?"

JOSEPH JR. No, it was an angel of God. God Almighty showed me the difference between an angel of light and Satan's angels. They called me a false and fallen prophet, but I am more in favor with my God this day than I ever was in all my life before.

DAVID. Is that the kind of God we have imagined for ourselves? A God who slays men, a God who justifies such principles?

MARY. *(Laughs)* Have you *read* the Bible?

DAVID. This is not the time of the Old Testament!

MARY. God is unchanging! It matters not what we imagine God to be, or what we want Him to be. God is who He is. His love, His truth, His righteousness is not bound by our societies, our private moralities and our philosophies. We are bound to Him, not the other way around. You are ignorant, my boy! Ignorant!

DAVID. I did not come here to be insulted.

MARY. And yet you have insulted me. You said that you came here wanting to know the truth, yet you close your ears! David, I told Joseph that I would not be his wife unless I had a witness.

JOSEPH JR. You will have a witness.

MARY. If God told you that, why does He not tell me?

DAVID. I've been asking myself that question quite a bit recently.

JOSEPH JR. Are you going to be a traitor?

MARY. I have never told a mortal, and shall never tell a mortal I had such a talk from a married man.

JOSEPH JR. Well, pray earnestly, for the angel said to me you should have a witness.

MARY. Well, Brigham Young was with me—he said if I had a witness, he wanted to know it.

DAVID. Brigham Young! This story suddenly becomes more suspicious!

MARY. Let go of your prejudices, David. Brigham Young was an emotional wreck over the principle. At the time, he liked it no more than you do now.

DAVID. I find that hard to swallow.

MARY. That's because you know the Brigham Young of now, not the Brigham Young of then. I assure you, he wasn't so full of confidence in the principle in those trying days.

DAVID. Go on. Go on with your story—I'm listening.

MARY. If ever a poor mortal prayed, I did. A few nights after that, an angel of the Lord came to me. A thrill went through me. I gazed upon the clothes and figure, but the eyes were like lightning. I was frightened almost to death for a moment. The angel leaned over me and the light was very great, although it was night.

DAVID. But—but the angel didn't say anything?

MARY. *(Laughs)* Hold on, my boy. Hold on. Your father came up to me the next Sabbath. He said:

THE FADING FLOWER

JOSEPH JR. Have you had a witness yet?

MARY. No.

JOSEPH JR. Well, the angel expressly told me you should have.

MARY. I have not had a witness, but I have seen something I have never seen before. I saw an angel and I was frightened almost to death. I did not speak.

DAVID. Are you expecting me to swallow this story, this fantastic story?

MARY. Listen. Learn to listen to your elders, and not be so fired up to interrupt and contradict. Your father studied a while and put his elbows on his knees and his face in his hands. He looked up and said:

JOSEPH JR. How could you have been such a coward? Did you not think to say, "Father help me?"

MARY ELIZABETH. I was weak.

JOSEPH JR. Well, if you had just said that, your mouth would have been opened, for that was an angel of the living God. He came to you with more knowledge, intelligence, and light than I ever dared reveal.

MARY. I was confused, you see, and asked your father, "Why then did he not speak to me?"

JOSEPH JR. You covered your face, and for this reason the angel was insulted.

DAVID. That's—that's a difficult story to believe.

MARY. Why? You've grown up with the stories of your father—the angels, the miracles, his visits from Christ and the Father. I am a living witness that those stories are true.

DAVID. If my father had so many other wives, why did he not have any children through them?

MARY. He did. I knew of three children. I think there's two living today, but they are not known as his children, as they go by other names. Perhaps there are more. You have brothers and sisters you know not of.

DAVID. I think I am finished. Good day, Mrs. Lightner.

MARY. You can call me Mary, if you wish.

DAVID. Mrs. Lightner will do for now.

MARY. I've seen him since, you know.

DAVID. Since when?

MARY. Since his death. Not long ago, in fact.

DAVID. What do you mean?

MARY. I was thinking about a sermon I had heard. All at once I looked up and they stood before me—Joseph, Hyrum, and Heber C. Kimball. They bowed to me about a dozen times or more. I went as to shake hands and then stopped and pinched myself to make sure I was awake. They saw my confusion, understood it, and laughed. I had no fear. As I went to shake hands with them, they bowed, smiled, and began to fade. They went like the sun sinks behind a mountain or a cloud. It gave me more courage and hope than I had ever had before.

DAVID. That, at least, is a nice image.

MARY. Do not let the truth knock you down for good, David.

(*Exit* DAVID. JOSEPH JR. *places his hand upon* MARY's *shoulder as they both look after him.*)

SCENE SEVEN

Enter CLARA, *who is sweeping. Enter* EMMA.

EMMA. Oh, Clara, I can do that—

CLARA. So can—

EMMA. I know you mean well, but you are young still.

CLARA. Sweeping isn't terribly difficult, Mother Smith.

EMMA. *(Pause)* Yes, you're right. I'm sorry, Clara.

(EMMA *turns to leave.*)

CLARA. Mother Smith?

(EMMA *stops. She turns and* CLARA *comes to her, giving her the broom.*)

CLARA. Here.

EMMA. No, Clara, I was just—

CLARA. While David is gone, I've decided to move in with my family.

EMMA. But, Clara, you know that you're welcome here.

CLARA. Am I?

EMMA. Of course, dear. Please reconsider—

CLARA. No, I don't think that I am welcome here.

EMMA. That's not fair—

CLARA. David's trusted in you and Joseph a great deal.

EMMA. A trust we've earned, I think.

CLARA. Man is supposed to leave father and mother and cleave to his wife.

EMMA. Clara, you ungrateful girl. We brought you into our care; we've helped you through your financial worries.

CLARA. If it wasn't for this family and this Church, we wouldn't be having financial worries! He'd be out there having real work!

EMMA. What would David think of you saying these things?

CLARA. Mother Smith, you loved your husband? You loved Joseph?

EMMA. You know I did.

CLARA. You knew that he was a prophet of God?

EMMA. I've had many witnesses. I cannot deny those.

CLARA. So you loved him, believed him, despite his faults? Despite whatever you may have seen as... wrong in his behavior?

EMMA. Joseph was a virtuous man.

CLARA. Emma? Was your husband a polygamist?

EMMA. He was a virtuous man! *(Pause)* You know, I think you're right. It's about time you stayed with your family.

CLARA. *(Hardening)* Yes, ma'am.

(Exit CLARA.*)*

SCENE NINE

JULIA *is occupying herself when* ALEXANDER *enters, quite agitated.*

ALEXANDER. Julia? What are you doing here?

JULIA. Well, good morning to you, too, Alex. I just got in last night.

ALEXANDER. Where's John?

JULIA. I—I've left John. I'm home for good now.

ALEXANDER. This is not a good time for our family, then.

JULIA. What's wrong?

ALEXANDER. David is home from Utah.

JULIA. Then tell him to come in!

ALEXANDER. Where's mother?

JULIA. Just in the other room. I'll go fetch her.

ALEXANDER. No, no, don't. He's in no frame of mind to talk to her.

JULIA. What do you mean?

ALEXANDER. Find a reason to go out back with her—

JULIA. What?

ALEXANDER. Please, just do it. I need to reason with him first.

(Enter EMMA.*)*

EMMA. What is the fuss all about? Can't a woman read in peace?

ALEXANDER. Mother, please, don't come in here.

EMMA. What? Why?

ALEXANDER. Trust me. It's very—

(Enter DAVID.)

EMMA. David? David!

(EMMA goes to embrace DAVID, but DAVID puts out his hand, fending her off.)

DAVID. Mother, why have you deceived us?

EMMA. David—what's wrong?

DAVID. I am not as I was.

(Blackout.)

SCENE NINE

Enter BIDAMON and JOSEPH III.

BIDAMON. You are a sight for sore eyes, Joseph. Please, take the boy out of here!

JOSEPH III. Nothing is decided yet, Major. I need to make sure David is as you have all written.

BIDAMON. Clara is nearly beside herself with fright.

JOSEPH III. Fright?

BIDAMON. We've been more than patient, Joseph, but this getting out of hand.

JOSEPH III. As I said, I need to see for myself.

BIDAMON. *(Seeing DAVID and CLARA approaching)* Well, here's your chance.

(Enter DAVID, CLARA *and* JULIA.*)*

DAVID. Get away from me!

CLARA. David, my dear—

DAVID. I am not your dear! I am not your anything!

CLARA. David!

DAVID. Joseph!

JOSEPH III. David, it is so nice to see you.

DAVID. You've brought a dark presence with you, Joseph, he sits above your head.

JULIA. David, please, talk sensibly.

DAVID. And you have one too, Julia!

BIDAMON. Do you see what I mean, Joseph?

DAVID. And Pa Bidamon—his is the largest!

JOSEPH III. David, are you troubled? We can talk about anything you—

DAVID. Do I dream or is the same subtle evil surrounding you that I have to contend with here? It seems so, at least.

JOSEPH III. David, you're not making a whole lot of sense—

DAVID. Clara took care of me when I was low, but she and I must be divorced.

JULIA. He's been saying that all day.

CLARA. He's shattering my feelings. *(Putting her hands on his face)* Oh my dear, dear David, you must see that you are not well.

DAVID. *(Becoming sincerely emotional)* I do feel tonight to say that my inner soul doth mourn over mine infirmities of flesh and spirit. It does seem as if the power to remain in that holy state of peace my heart once knew has departed. My talk is astounding to myself and I marvel whence it cometh. As sure as I live, it proceeds not from my heart, nor is it David that speaks thus.

JOSEPH III. He's possessed.

JULIA. What?

BIDAMON. No, no, don't be foolish. This is clinical.

JOSEPH III. He was involved in spiritualism in Utah. With his sensitive nature—

BIDAMON. Ridiculous! Get those notions out of your head.

JOSEPH III. Lyman's the one who did this, him and his séances.

DAVID. *(To* JOSEPH III*)* Nothing grieves me more than the thought that one so long beaten by the storm of the world and evil should find so broken a tooth, so sore a broken joint on which to lean.

(Enter EMMA.*)*

EMMA. Joseph, you're here! Thank heaven.

DAVID. *(To* EMMA*)* It is gone, Mother, the unity that existed between you and Joseph. Peace be with you. You did not mean that I was a post.

EMMA. *(Gently grabbing his arm)* Come, David, come into the garden with me.

DAVID. *(Recoiling)* You were under their influence too much! I never say grace comfort you any longer. Do not imagine but that I would say it if grace were accommodating. If ever the scale turns and I conquer circumstances, I will remember you better.

CLARA. No, no, David, I think your mother is right. The garden will do you good—you love the garden.

DAVID. I want a divorce! You have been unfaithful—I know it!

CLARA. David, please, don't talk like that. I love you—I would never do any such thing.

DAVID. Unfaithful!

CLARA. David—

DAVID. I want a divorce!

CLARA. *(Crying)* David, don't! Stop it!

JULIA. Clara, he doesn't mean it.

CLARA. He's ravaging my heart.

JULIA. *(Holding her)* Hush, dear, hush.

DAVID. Within and apart sit my spirit with white wings, and robes, and mourns at the state of her broken tabernacle, and sighs at the storm about and around.

CLARA. David, David, be quiet. Your words are so mad and so beautiful—your old wine put into a wretched new bottle! It's but a bright glimpse of you smothered in dark robes!

DAVID. I want a divorce.

CLARA. David!

EMMA. Julia, take Clara out.

CLARA. David, you've got to get better! For me, for your son.

JULIA. Come now, Clara—

CLARA. Show me some hope that you are going to get better.

JULIA. Clara—

CLARA. Please, show me!

DAVID. I want a divorce.

JULIA. Let's go.

(JULIA and CLARA exit, CLARA weeping.)

BIDAMON. I'll go with them.

(Exit BIDAMON.)

EMMA. Joseph—

JOSEPH III. I know, Mother. Now, David—

DAVID. Mesmerism allows people control over each other. Two people see each other admire each and they will assume expression intermediate between the two, and the more compact or strongly mental will control the other.

JOSEPH III. See that, Mother—it's the spiritualism.

DAVID. Undertones and subvoices. The subvoice can talk and the eyesight see and ear hear at great distance from the body.

JOSEPH III. David, please, come listen to me.

DAVID. Get away, Brother Smith—they're coming.

JOSEPH III. David, look at me—

(DAVID *runs, puts his face between his knees and shouts.*)

DAVID. I told you that they would!

EMMA. David! Stop it, stop it, my boy. This is going on too long.

DAVID. Rapidly revolving machinery will control people in this manner, pass them out around and through each other and tear them to pieces. Sometimes people suffer terribly in this.

JOSEPH III. *(Grabbing* DAVID's *hands)* David, I'm going to take you to my house for a little while. You'll be able to spend some time with me and my family. We're going to try to make you better. Do you understand me?

DAVID. This has been a day of awful visitation. The air has been filled with iron ore and steam and it so fearfully acidulant.

JOSEPH III. David, did you understand what I told you?

DAVID. Joseph—you desire me to die. Because I can never tolerate your religion in private. You desire my suicide!

JOSEPH III. No, David, I love you! I want the best for you!

(EMMA *comes and embraces her son, both of them sinking to the ground.* DAVID *melts into her arms, weeping.*)

EMMA. We love you, my darling. You are my dear, my sensitive boy.

DAVID. *(With sudden lucidity)* Mother, if ever I have added sorrow to your heart, it has doubly troubled mine. I know your reward in Heaven is sure—whatever mine may be, white robes and crown are awaiting you. There are many suffering worse than we have suffered. It is a good thing to walk among these; one learns contentment there.

EMMA. David! My dear David...

DAVID. Well, Dear Mother, remember me as if I had been all I might have been. I am your boy.

(EMMA *weeps, cradling* DAVID.)

JOSEPH III. How it will terminate, God alone knows.

SCENE TEN

David's Chamber behind the waterfall. DAVID *sits there, quietly.* JOSEPH JR. *sits next to him, unseen, but comforting* DAVID. *Enter* EMMA.

EMMA. David! You mustn't worry me like that. (DAVID *doesn't reply or acknowledge* EMMA) I knew I'd find you here. (DAVID *closes his eyes*) David—oh, David, look at what they've done to you.

DAVID. David's Chamber.

EMMA. Yes, this is your place. It will carry your name forever.

DAVID. It was supposed to be my secret place. No more secrets.

EMMA. David, I—we've made a decision. You know that you are sick, David.

DAVID. No more secrets.

EMMA. I took care of you—Joseph took care of you—for ten years, he did. We're looking for somewhere—we're trying to find a new place for you to live.

DAVID. I'll go out into the world. The wanderer, outward bound.

EMMA. You're sick, David. I—I can't—my strength is gone. But these people will be able to take care of you. They'll protect you.

DAVID. Stone and water—

EMMA. David, do you understand what I'm telling you?

DAVID. Yes, Mother. Incarcerated in rock.

EMMA. No, David, you don't—

JOSEPH JR. Thou shalt bear a child, and though he be incarcerated in solid rock, yet he shall come out and make his mark in the world. Call his name David.

DAVID. I'll make my mark.

> *(Lights go off of DAVID.)*

SCENE ELEVEN

> EMMA *sits alone. Enter* PARLEY P. PRATT JR.

PARLEY. Mrs. Smith—I mean, Mrs. Bidamon.

EMMA. Who are you?

PARLEY. Pardon me, your husband told me you were in here. I took the liberty. I am Parley P. Pratt.

EMMA. Excuse me, but I was well acquainted with Parley Pratt, and you are not him.

PARLEY. Excuse me. Parley P. Pratt Jr.

EMMA. Ah. Another "junior."

PARLEY. Yours and my father's generation left us quite the legacy. We hope to emulate it.

EMMA. We already lived it for you. Let that suffice.

> *(Enter* THOMAS B. MARSH, JUNIOR. *He is playing out a totally separate scene with* EMMA. *It is important that it is made clear that these are separate events in* EMMA'*s life that are playing out at the same time.)*

MARSH. Mrs. Bidamon?

EMMA. Another interviewer?

MARSH. I am Thomas B. Marsh's son.

EMMA. Another son.

MARSH. Yes, ma'am.

PARLEY AND MARSH. You knew my father well.

EMMA. I could never forget him. Parley, when I heard about...about your father's murder...

PARLEY. That's been many years ago, now.

EMMA. The last time I saw him was Nauvoo.

MARSH. Did you hear that my father returned to the Utah Church?

EMMA. If your father hadn't apostatized, he would have been the leader of the Utah Church now instead of that man.

MARSH. Is it important who leads the Church as long as the Lord leads that man?

> *(Enter* JOSEPH SMITH III *and* ALEXANDER. *Again, this is a separate piece of time being played simultaneously with the two other scenes.)*

JOSEPH III. Mother, are you ready?

EMMA. The interview?

PARLEY AND MARSH. Do you mind if I ask you a few questions?

ALEXANDER. Mother, if you don't feel up to it—

EMMA. I'm up to it.

PARLEY. Do you believe that your husband, Joseph Smith, died true to his profession?

EMMA. I believe he was everything he professed to be.

JOSEPH III. What of the truth of Mormonism?

EMMA. I know Mormonism to be the truth, and believe the Church to have been established by divine direction. In writing for your father I frequently wrote day after day, often sitting at the table close by him and dictating hour after hour with nothing between us.

PARLEY. Did he receive the plates from which he claimed to have translated the Book of Mormon?

EMMA. Yes, they lay in a box under our bed for months, but I never felt at liberty to look at them.

ALEXANDER. Had he not a book or manuscript from which he read, dictated to you?

EMMA. He had neither manuscript nor book to read from.

ALEXANDER. Could he not have had, and you not know it?

EMMA. If he had anything of the kind, he could not have concealed it from me.

JOSEPH III. Are you sure that he had the plates at the time you were writing for him?

EMMA. The plates often lay on the table without any attempt at concealment, wrapped in a small, linen tablecloth, which I had given him to fold them in. I once felt of the plates, as they lay thus on my table, tracing their outline and shape. They seemed to be pliable like thick paper, and would rustle with a metallic sound when the edges were moved by a thumb, as one does sometimes thumb the edges of a book.

ALEXANDER. Could not Father have dictated the Book of Mormon to Oliver Cowdery and the others who wrote for him after having first written it, or having first read it out of some book?

EMMA. Joseph Smith could neither write nor dictate a coherent and well-written letter, let alone the Book of Mormon.

MARSH. What of polygamy?

PARLEY. Did he receive the revelation on plural marriage?

EMMA. Not to my knowledge.

PARLEY. Mrs. Bidamon, people have been imprisoned for this principle, have... died for this principle. My father died as a martyr for polygamy. He was shot by his plural wife's former husband, out of revenge. I repeat, did Joseph Smith Jr., your husband, receive the revelation on plural marriage?

EMMA. Not to my knowledge.

MARSH. Why did you use your influence to have your son installed as the President of the Reorganization, knowing, as you must have, that the men who would confer upon him his authority were apostates, and some of them had been cut off from the Church?

EMMA. I did not influence the men who came to my sons to invite them to lead their group.

MARSH. Nor did you ultimately stop them.

EMMA. Brigham Young entirely ignored my family! In our time of grief, he did not give us the proper consideration! We not only deserved recognition, but representation within the Church. My son, Joseph, not Brigham Young, ought to be President of the Church. It is his right.

PARLEY. Mrs. Bidamon—

MARSH. Mrs. Smith—

PARLEY. Emma, why didn't you come West with the rest of the Saints?

EMMA. You may think that I was not a very good Saint not to go West, but I had a home here and did not go because I did not know what I should have there.

JOSEPH III. Mother—

ALEXANDER. Mother—

JOSEPH III. Mother, what about the revelation on polygamy?

ALEXANDER. Did Joseph Smith have anything like it?

JOSEPH III. What of spiritual wifery?

EMMA. There was no revelation on either polygamy or spiritual wives.

ALEXANDER. Did he have any wives other than yourself?

EMMA. He had no other wife but me, nor to my knowledge did ever have.

JOSEPH III. Did he not hold marital relation with women other than yourself?

EMMA. He did not have improper relations with any woman that ever came to my knowledge. I know that he had no other wife of wives than myself, in any sense, either spiritual or otherwise.

JOSEPH III. Thank you, Mother. You have given us the answers we needed.

(*Exit* JOSEPH III *and* ALEXANDER. EMMA *looks up at* PARLEY, *vulnerable.*)

EMMA. What if...what if my family and I were to someday...what if we were to return to the Church in Utah? How do you think we would be received?

PARLEY. (*Warmly*) You would be received with open arms by President Young and the whole body of the Church. You'd want for nothing to make you comfortable and your family happy.

EMMA. I...oh, how I wish time could go back on its axle. How I wish I could—oh, Joseph—I miss him so much. If he were here, perhaps this could all be worked out.

PARLEY. Good night, Mrs. Smith.

(*Exit* PARLEY. THOMAS *is the only one who remains. He approaches her.*)

EMMA. Any other questions, Mr. Marsh?

MARSH. Was Joseph Smith a polygamist?

EMMA. My husband—

MARSH. Did he practice Celestial Marriage?

EMMA. I—He—

MARSH. Please, Sister Smith. I know this is very hard for you, but is it not time that the truth come out plainly and without dispute?

(*At this* EMMA *breaks down, weeping.*)

EMMA. You don't understand.... You don't understand—

MARSH. Then help me understand.

EMMA. You must excuse me from answering directly.

MARSH. Why?

EMMA. Because my son Joseph is the leader of the Reorganized Church.

MARSH. This is for him, then?

EMMA. Excuse me—please, excuse me—

(THOMAS *exits and* EMMA *breaks down, weeping.* EMMA *turns and for the first time in the play* EMMA *"sees"* JOSEPH JR. *At first,* JOSEPH JR. *says nothing.*)

EMMA. Joseph? (*Pause.* EMMA *clutches her beads*) See? I still have them. The gold beads you gave me. (JOSEPH *tries to approach* EMMA, *but she retreats slightly*) Why? Why all this trouble? (JOSEPH *doesn't answer*) Please, Joseph, some sort of indication, some sort of answer. (JOSEPH *doesn't answer*) It dominates the conversation.... You do realize that, don't you? You...you died for the Book of Mormon. You died for your revelations and your visions and your intimate friendship with Providence. The cowards killed you hiding behind their mobs and their preachers and their torches, but your soul stood bold and immortal before them. You had a good death, Joseph, protecting your people, your...family. All of your family. But they will think...they will think that it all came down to that divisive principle. Is that what you want your legacy to be? (JOSEPH *approaches* EMMA, EMMA *once again retreats*) No, no, hold on. When I sat in Mr. Knight's wagon at the bottom of that hill all those years ago, my mind was one chaotic jumble. You were up on that hill, claiming that you were talking to an angel, and that you would bring down gold plates—gold! Reformed Egyptian, you told me! Ancient American prophets, you told me! And the most astounding aspect is that I believed you—I still believed you. I believe you still. For when you came down off that hill you had a bundle in which you said were the plates, and a broken thumb from protecting it from the men who were waiting to catch you. You went to such trouble, your eyes were so honest, you...you laid your breast against the musket time and again for your stories. When I tore the tar and feathers off your naked flesh; when I saw you for the first time in several months after being imprisoned in that hell-hole in Missouri; when I saw you leave on your horse to Carthage, knowing you were going to your death—even when I didn't know it...How could I ever doubt you? How could they think that I could *ever* doubt you! Not the Book of Mormon, not your visions, not your miracles. But...but *this*. After everything, why do their questions always lead back to polygamy? It's a minor footnote compared to what God was able to accomplish through you. But what if they forgot? What if we were able to clear your name of that smear and focus their eyes on the real truth? Would that not be worth it? Would that not bring the *important* truths to the forefront?

>(JOSEPH JR. *doesn't answer.* EMMA's *eyes plead with him for a moment, before* JOSEPH JR. *approaches* EMMA. *This time* EMMA *doesn't retreat, but flinches slightly as* JOSEPH JR. *lightly, lovingly touches her face.* EMMA *then relinquishes and collapses into* JOSEPH JR.'s *arms, weeping.*)

EMMA. I feel like I'm just fading away, like blossoms being blown off an apple tree. Oh, Joseph, please, please come for me.

>(JOSEPH JR. *gently draws back from the embrace, kisses* EMMA *and steps back into the shadows. Enter* JULIA. JULIA *takes* EMMA *and undresses her down to a nightgown. She brings* EMMA *to a bed, close to death.* JULIA *sits next to her, knitting, or reading, or some other quiet activity.* JOSEPH JR. *enters, standing out of the way, but watching intently.*)

EMMA. Still there, Julia?

JULIA. Yes, Mother. Go back to sleep. You need your rest.

EMMA. I'm glad you came home—are you still a Catholic?

JULIA. Yes.

EMMA. I get mixed up. I didn't like John much—he made you a Catholic. That drinking—oh, that drinking. Neither of us seemed to have luck with our husbands—

JULIA. Don't talk too much. Save your strength.

EMMA. I'm glad you're home.

JULIA. Mother... Mother, I have something to tell you.

EMMA. Yes?

JULIA. The sores that you were worried about on my breast and back... I have... I am very sick.

EMMA. You'll be following me soon, then.

JULIA. Perhaps.

EMMA. Your father was a prophet, Julia.

JULIA. I... I know. You're speaking too much. You need to rest.

EMMA. Will you visit David at the Asylum before you go?

JULIA. I would like to.

EMMA. Promise me that you'll bring him some clematis or dahlias. Get them there, so they don't fade too quickly. Don't squeeze them too tight.

JULIA. I promise.

EMMA. Have I told you my dream yet?

JULIA. What dream?

EMMA. I had it a couple of weeks ago.

JULIA. No, you didn't tell me about any dream.

EMMA. A vision. God finally gave me a vision. I told the maid.

JULIA. Tell me about it.

EMMA. Joseph came to me. He said:

JOSEPH JR. Emma, come with me. It is time for you to come with me.

EMMA. I put on my bonnet and my shawl and went with him. We went into a mansion, and he showed me through the different apartments. We went into a nursery and there was a cradle—

JULIA. Yes?

EMMA. I knew my baby, my Don Carlos that was taken from me. I caught Don Carlos up in my arms and wept. I then turned to Joseph and said, "Joseph, where are the rest of my children?"

JOSEPH JR. Emma, be patient and you shall have all your children.

EMMA. Then—oh, so sweet—

JULIA. What happened, Mother?

EMMA. Then I saw behind Joseph a personage of light. I saw Jesus Christ.

JULIA. Mother—oh, thank the Lord—

EMMA. I do, my dear. I do. But—

JULIA. Mother?

EMMA. Where are the other children?

JULIA. No, no, it's not time—

EMMA. Where are my children?

JULIA. Alexander! Joseph! Where are you?

   (ALEXANDER *enters.*)

ALEXANDER. What? What is it?

JULIA. Mother. She's fading away.

ALEXANDER. No—

EMMA. (*Seeing* JOSEPH JR.) Joseph—

ALEXANDER. She wants Joseph. Joseph, where are you?

EMMA. Joseph—Joseph—Joseph—

JULIA. No, no, it's not her son she wants. She sees him.

ALEXANDER. What?

   (*Enter* JOSEPH III.)

JOSEPH III. Mother!

   (*All three of them crowd around her bed, but* EMMA *rises out of the bed. They act as if she is still within it.*)

ALEXANDER. She's gone.

(EMMA *exits with* JOSEPH JR.)

SCENE TWELVE

JULIA *rises, crying, with* JOSEPH III *and* ALEXANDER *following behind her.*

ALEXANDER. Julia!

JULIA. Please, just leave me alone...

ALEXANDER. Now, more than ever, we need each other. Let's stand united—

JULIA. United! We're all tossed into the wind like sand!

(ALEXANDER *stops* JULIA *and holds her by the shoulders, looking her straight in her eyes.*)

ALEXANDER. Julia, don't let go of us and we won't let go of you.

JULIA. Alex, with Mother dead and David gone, I'm an outsider now—in a sense I always was.

ALEXANDER. Ridiculous. You're a Smith.

(JULIA *melts into* ALEXANDER'*s arms and unburdens more emotion.*)

JULIA. If my birth mother hadn't died, I would be a Murdock, not a Smith. I sometimes think about that—I would be out West right now, with my fath—with John Murdock. I would be a Brighamite. Perhaps a Brighamite's wife—a plural wife...

JOSEPH III. I don't want to hear any more talk like that.

(JULIA, *hardening, gently takes herself out of* ALEXANDER'*s arms and stares coldly at* JOSEPH III.)

JULIA. I can talk how I want.

JOSEPH III. For once, be proud that you're a daughter of Joseph Smith!

(*This stuns* JULIA *and* ALEXANDER.)

ALEXANDER. Joseph!

(JULIA *slaps* JOSEPH III.)

ALEXANDER. Julia!

JULIA. Alex, can I have a moment alone with Joe?

ALEXANDER. There's no way I'm leaving you two alone with this kind of—

JOSEPH III. Leave, Alex.

(ALEX *exits, ruffled.*)

JULIA. I loved Father.

JOSEPH III. Then why haven't you stayed true to him, to his cause?

JULIA. You mean your cause?

JOSEPH III. They are one and the same!

JULIA. I have my doubts on that point.

JOSEPH III. Why can't I have your support in this? I have Alexander's support, I had Mother's, I had David's—

JULIA. You had David's support until he went to Utah.

JOSEPH III. David isn't accountable for how he—

JULIA. David was the only one of us who was courageous enough to go after the truth.

JOSEPH III. The truth! What David found in Utah was not the truth!

JULIA. Have *you* gone and talked to the people David did? Have *you* gone against your own instincts to hazard a clearer picture? Have *you* searched and pried and dug like David did?

JOSEPH III. I've talked to Mother and she contradicted all of that!

JULIA. Do you think Mother was really going to go against her oldest living son, especially to defend a principle that brought her so much heartache?

JOSEPH III. I can't believe we're having this conversation.

JULIA. You ought to believe it!

JOSEPH III. So what are you insinuating? That—that the Brighamites are right?

JULIA. No. Maybe. Honestly, I don't know.

JOSEPH III. Julia—there was once a day when I could not even think of our father practicing plural marriage. It was simply not an option. But—

JULIA. But? Did you just say—?

JOSEPH III. Look, Julia, I'm not a simpleton, all right? Yes, yes, I have fought and struggled against the idea my whole adult life, and I still believe—but, if I'm wrong and he did practice polygamy—

JULIA. Am I really hearing this?

JOSEPH III. If Father taught polygamy, he was wrong!

JULIA. *(Pause)* You hypocrite. If you believe that Father could have practiced polygamy, then why this whole posture to the world?

JOSEPH III. Julia, a mantle has been given to me, an opportunity—

JULIA. Joe, either you believe father was a prophet or not. If not, then by all means, go back to your farming, to your law books, to your old way of life and stop dragging in people like Alex and David and Clara and Mother to bear the brunt of the storm for you!

JOSEPH III. I am part of something much bigger than any of us now. We have an opportunity to bring the Gospel of Jesus Christ to the world! To be His emissaries!

JULIA. We are not His emissaries if we tell the truth on one subject and then lie on the next.

JOSEPH III. Julia, we can do great good, but we must be practical. If we insist on prying too much into complicated matters that are better left buried—well, then we'll all end up like poor David, blinded by the fire.

JULIA. David did not lose his sanity because he was told the truth in the end, David lost his sanity because he was not told the truth from the beginning. If he hadn't had a false world constructed around him, he would have been able to endure the real one.

JOSEPH III. Do you realize the great offense you're giving to our Mother when you say such things?

JULIA. I am utterly tired of all of us placing the burden squarely on Mother! She had enough burdens without us giving her ours!

JOSEPH III. And that's why—

JULIA. That's why when it was our turn to be strong, we utterly failed her. The tragedy is that we never let her be fallible.

JOSEPH III. Julia, this Church can't fail. We must do everything in our power to support it, we must not let anything, true or not, prevent God's Church from progressing.

JULIA. Truth is God's Church. The Truth will make us free.

JOSEPH III. We can't lose the influence we've already gained!

JULIA. Influence?

JOSEPH III. I am determined to see the cause of Christ become the mightiest organization upon this earth!

JULIA. God's kingdom is not of this earth! What is this about? God's Church? Or your own good name?

JOSEPH III. Don't you see? I've inherited both. Father's Church and his name are now both literally mine. Whatever tarnishes Father's Church tarnishes my Church, and whatever tarnishes Father's name tarnishes my name! (JULIA *looks* JOSEPH III *over and then turns to exit.* JOSEPH III *stops her with his voice*) Julia, where are you going?

JULIA. I think both of us can see that this is fruitless.

JOSEPH III. No, please, just keep listening and I'll show you why I'm right. Please come back, Julia. It's not too late to step into the light.

JULIA. Are you sure that it's the light?

JOSEPH III. God satisfied me long ago that we have more light than the Brighamites.

JULIA. I don't care about any sort of "ites." What I care about is making myself right with God. Where he leads, I will follow, but I don't think that will be here or in the West. I think my path is much shorter than that.

JOSEPH III. What do you mean?

JULIA. I don't have very much time, Joseph.

JOSEPH III. Of course you do. We all do. We are not getting so old as all that.

JULIA. I'm going to see David tomorrow.

JOSEPH III. What?

JULIA. He missed the funeral. Everything.

JOSEPH III. You know how difficult it would have been to—

JULIA. We should have found a way.

JOSEPH III. Julia—

JULIA. I am going to see David tomorrow. I hope you and Alex will come with me.

JOSEPH III. I'm not sure that's—

JULIA. What are you afraid of?

JOSEPH III. *(Pause)* I'll come. Anything to please you, Jute.

JULIA. *(Smiling at her old nickname)* It's good to hear you call me that again.

(Goes to exit, but then turns one last time) The truth is a pesky thing, Joe. No matter how deep we try to submerge it, it will always rise back to the top.

(JULIA *and* JOSEPH III *consider each other, and then* JULIA *exits. After a slight, thoughtful pause,* JOSEPH III *exits.)*

SCENE THIRTEEN

DAVID *enters, pantomiming gardening, humming softly. Enter* JOSEPH III, JULIA, *and* ALEXANDER. *They are out of* DAVID's *hearing at first.*

JOSEPH III. I'm not sure I can do this.

ALEXANDER. We have to.

JULIA. Look at him. He looks so peaceful.... Like nothing has changed.

JOSEPH III. We can't keep in mind the old David. He's something new, something different.

JULIA. Well, I, for one, will not be a coward when it comes to my own flesh and blood.

(JULIA *goes over and starts gardening with* DAVID.)

DAVID. Good morning.

JULIA. Good morning, David.

DAVID. I know you, don't I?

JULIA. Yes, you do.

DAVID. You're Julia. My sister.

JULIA. Very good, David.

DAVID. "Oh, ever thus from childhood's hour, I have seen my fondest hopes decay; I never nursed a tree or flower, but it was the first to fade and die."

JULIA. (*Pause. Trying to restrain deep emotion*) You remember that?

DAVID. Remember what?

(ALEXANDER *comes and starts gardening as well.*)

ALEXANDER. The doctors—they say that they let you garden here now. That's wonderful. They say you're making progress.

JULIA. We've brought you seeds. New flowers to plant.

DAVID. Clematis and dahlias.

ALEXANDER. Yes. Your favorite.

DAVID. Are they? I suppose they are.

(DAVID *pantomimes tearing up a flower by its roots. He throws it to the ground.*)

JULIA. David, you mustn't do that.

DAVID. "Oh, ever thus from childhood's hour, I have seen my fondest hopes decay; I never nursed a tree or flower, but it was the first to fade and die."

JULIA. No. We must take care of the flowers as long as we can. Appreciate their beauty while we have them.

(DAVID *begins humming again.*)

ALEXANDER. The doctors said you're gentle, harmless—you were always harmless, until you first lost your... until you became sick.

DAVID. Sick. Am I sick? I don't feel sick.

JULIA. We miss you.

DAVID. I like the flowers. But we're uprooted.... How did we become uprooted?

(*David tears out another flower.* JOSEPH III *comes and kneels beside* DAVID, *looking him in the eyes.*)

JOSEPH III. You were supposed to be our great advocate in the Church. I wanted you to be my counselor.

DAVID. Clematis and dahlias. Claras and Davids. Clara... Clara...

JOSEPH III. We love you, David.

(DAVID *tears out another flower.*)

DAVID. Uprooted. Now it's fading. Dying. But this one—(*Regarding a still-planted flower*)—this one's still alive. But it will die, too. Winter will kill it.

(DAVID *starts humming again.* ALEXANDER *and* JOSEPH III *glance at each other nervously, but* JULIA *remains focused on* DAVID.)

DAVID. Where is mother?

JOSEPH III. David...we wrote you about mother...

DAVID. Where is mother?

JOSEPH III. Mother was sick for a long time. Quietly and peacefully, she went to her eternal sleep. We buried her over the hillside, there among the locusts and lilacs. It was such that...we could not come or send for you, or we would have done so.

DAVID. Where is mother?

JOSEPH III. David, please...

JULIA. *(Understanding* DAVID's *real question)* Mother's in heaven, with father.

DAVID. That's what I thought.

(DAVID *goes back to gardening.*)

JOSEPH III. May I garden with you, David?

DAVID. Sing. All of you must sing.

JULIA. What song, David?

(*As he continues to garden,* DAVID *begins to sing a song which he had written for the RLDS Hymnbook. As they, too, garden, his siblings reticent and affected at first, each relent and sing as well.*)

DAVID. Let us shake off the coals from our garments,

    And arise in the strength of the Lord,

    Let us break off the yoke of bondage,

    and be free in the joy of his word:

JULIA. For the pebble has dropped in the water,

    And the waves circle round with the shock:

DAVID AND JULIA. Shall we anchor our barks in the center,

    Or drift out and be wrecked on the rock?

DAVID, JULIA, AND ALEXANDER. Thank the Lord for the plan he has given,

That will render us as pure as a child,
That will change this cold world into heaven.

DAVID, JULIA, ALEXANDER, AND JOSEPH III. By his Spirit so holy and mild,
And the hope of a portion of Zion,
Shall cheer us till trials are o'er—
Let us anchor our barks in the center,
And be safe from the rocks on the shore.

(Fade to black.)

THE END

Kathryn Laycock Little as Emma Smith and Amos Omer as David Hyrum Smith in New Play Project's production of *The Fading Flower*, May–June 2009. *Photo by Naoma Wilkinson.*

William McAllister as Joseph Smith Jr. and Amos Omer as David Hyrum Smith in New Play Project's production of *The Fading Flower*, May–June 2009. *Photo by Naoma Wilkinson.*

Jamie Dawn Denison as Julia Smith and Kathryn Laycock Little as Emma Smith in New Play Project's production of *The Fading Flower*, May–June 2009. *Photo by Christian Cragun.*

Left to right: Amos Omer as David Hyrum Smith, Jamie Dawn Denison as Julia Smith, Rachel Baird as Clara Hartshorn, Kathryn Laycock Little as Emma Smith, and Mahonri Stewart as Lewis Bidamon in the New Play Project's production of *The Fading Flower*, May–June 2009. Photo by Christian Cragun.

Left to right: David Dixon as Thomas Marsh Jr., Arisael Rivera as Alexander Smith, Kathryn Laycock Little as Emma Smith, Adam Argyle as Joseph Smith III, and Brennan Cartwright as Parley P. Pratt Jr. in New Play Project's production of *The Fading Flower*, May–June 2009. Photo by Christian Cragun.

Left to right: Mary Heaps as Mary Elizabeth Rollins Lightner, Heather Jones as Eliza R. Snow, and Sarah-Lucy Hill as Helen Mar Kimball in New Play Project's production of *The Fading Flower*, May–June 2009. *Photo by Christian Cragun.*

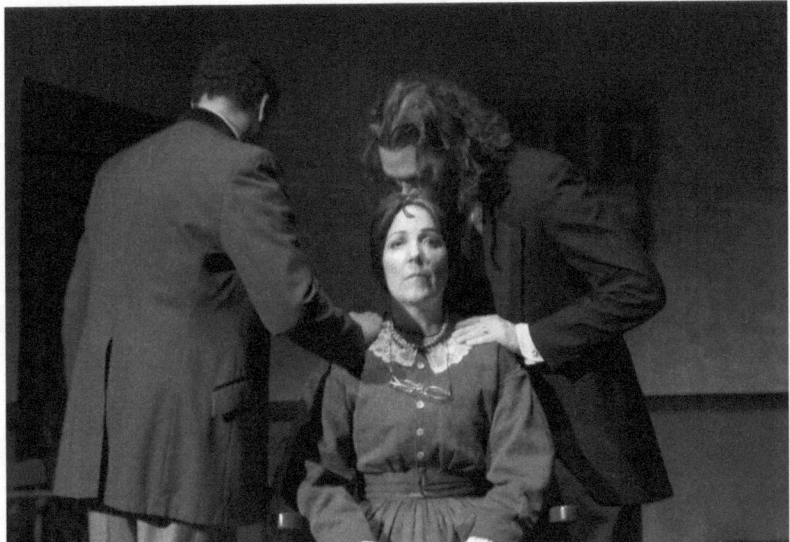

Left to right: Arisael Rivera as Alexander Smith, Kathryn Laycock Little as Emma Smith, and Adam Argyle as Joseph Smith III in New Play Project's production of *The Fading Flower*, May–June 2009. *Photo by Christian Cragun.*

Left to right: Brennan Cartwright as Samuel Smith Jr., Kathryn Laycock Little as Emma Smith, and Alex Barlow as Joseph F. Smith in New Play Project's production of *The Fading Flower*, May–June 2009. *Photo by Christian Cragun.*

William McAllister as Joseph Smith Jr. and Kathryn Laycock Little as Emma Smith in New Play Project's production of *The Fading Flower*, May–June 2009. *Photo by Christian Cragun.*

Adam Stallard as Amasa Lyman and Amos Omer as David Hyrum Smith in New Play Project's production of *The Fading Flower*, May–June 2009. *Photo by Christian Cragun.*

William McAllister as Joseph Smith Jr., Kathryn Laycock Little as Emma Smith, and Adam Stallard as Frederick Smith in New Play Project's production of *The Fading Flower*, May–June 2009. Photo by Christian Cragun.

Rachel Baird as Clara Hartshorn and Amos Omer as David Hyrum Smith in New Play Project's production of *The Fading Flower*, May–June 2009. *Photo by Christian Cragun.*

Swallow the Sun

Production History

Swallow the Sun first premiered on May 16, 2008, at the Provo Theater by New Play Project. Mahonri Stewart directed the first production, with costume design by Anne Marie Stewart, lighting design by Melissa Leilani Larson, and music provided by Brian Randall. The original cast was as follows:

C. S. "Jack" Lewis: C. Adam Stallard

Paddy Moore: Jeff Bond

Janie Moore: Tatum Langton

Maureen Moore: Rachael Stewart

Albert Lewis: James Goldberg

Warnie Lewis: Amos Omer

J. R. R. Tolkien: David Dixon

Hugo Dyson: Matthew Price Davies

Arthur Greeves: Cole Hooley

Owen Barfield: Will McCallister

John "Doc" Askins: Eric "C" Heaps

Mary "Smudge" Wibelin: Jana Stubbs

As this is a play of fathers and sons, on earth and in Heaven,

it is dedicated to my own father and son:

to George Owen Stewart, who has always been such a support morally, spiritually, materially, and lovingly; and Hyrum Irving Stewart, who was born right before this play was, and whose very initials are inscribed in the play's last word.

*I am a wolf that follows the sun
And I will catch him ere day be done.*

—C.S. Lewis, "Spirits in Bondage"

When the time comes to you at which you will be forced at last to utter the speech which has lain at the center of your soul for years, which you have, all that time, idiot-like, been saying over and over, you'll not talk about joy of words. I saw well why the gods do not speak to us openly, nor let us answer. Till that word can be dug out of us, why should they hear the babble that we think we mean? How can they meet us face to face till we have faces?

—C.S. Lewis, *Till We Have Faces*

Swallow the Sun

Act One

SCENE ONE

We see C. S. "JACK" LEWIS *in a World War I O.T.C. (Officer Training Corps) uniform on a bed, writing in a notebook.* JACK *is originally from Ireland, but speaks in a polished British accent.* JACK *begins the play in his very early twenties. Enter* EDWARD "PADDY" MOORE, *an Irish young man who has retained his native accent and who is about* JACK's *age.* PADDY *rummages through his things and pulls out a copy of a book of Tennyson's poetry, flops on his bed, and begins reading.* JACK *looks up, surprised.*

JACK. Paddy?

PADDY. Yes, Jack?

JACK. What is that you're doing?

PADDY. It's called reading, Jack. A curious habit I picked up when I was younger.

JACK. Well, obviously you're reading. What I meant—

PADDY. I've been trying to kick the habit for a number of years now, but then I go through these terrible withdrawals. Headaches, longings, nervous twitching—

(JACK *goes over to* PADDY *and swipes the book out of his hand.*)

JACK. Egad, I was right! Tennyson, no less!

PADDY. Here now, what's the fuss!

JACK. I must apologize, Paddy—I hadn't figured that you were the type. You usually can tell just by their daily habits and what not.

PADDY. Jack, really, give it back.

JACK. You're a bookish fellow, aren't you, Paddy?! You're an intellectual!

PADDY. Please, Jack, I don't want to hear any sniggering from you about it.

JACK. Sniggering? Oh no, surely not! Here. *(JACK gives PADDY his book back and then goes to his own things and picks out a book of his own, from which he starts reading.)*

"I yearn'd for warmth and colour which I found

In Lancelot—now I see what thou art,

Not Lancelot, nor another. Is there none

Will tell the King I love him tho' so late?"

PADDY. Idylls of the King!

JACK. Oh, wonderful! Here I thought you some childish boy, not fit for decent, sophisticated company. But here, among soldiers who drop their h's and spit on the floor, here I find an intellectual for a roommate! A reader of poetry, no less. This is grand!

PADDY. I've suddenly become interesting, have I?

JACK. Infinitely interesting!

PADDY. Why, Jack, you're a snob, aren't you?

JACK. Most incorrigibly so! Look now, Paddy, we all know that there are different groups among us—it's an unpleasant fact that must be faced. There are the "rankers." They're good enough—won't lie to you, won't cheat you, they clean themselves up and will give you a friendly face—but they're naive.

PADDY. Really, Jack—

JACK. Then there are the "cads and fools." Vicious lot, really. Can't get their minds to anything higher than women, alcohol, and dirty jokes.

PADDY. And then what are we, Jack?

JACK. "The public school and varsity men."

PADDY. So we're the educated, the readers, the intellectuals, the crème de la crème?

JACK. Exactly.

PADDY. Well, at least you haven't any pretensions about your pretensions.

JACK. Ah, Paddy, you may hide behind the bashful humility, but you know I'm right. You're one of my type of men. May I make a suggestion, however?

PADDY. If it is as entertaining as the rest of your talk.

JACK. Try and lose the accent.

PADDY. Pardon me?

JACK. Oh, there's no shame in being Irish. I was born in Belfast, myself, and will announce that to anyone I meet. My father still has the accent rather bad, however. But my brother and I knocked it out of ourselves in school. Didn't want people to think of us as common potato farmers.

PADDY. I'll pretend you don't know how offensive you're being.

JACK. You've already lost a lot of it—you certainly don't go around calling everyone "lad." That's a good start. Your problem is inflection, not word choice, which is a jolly good sign.

PADDY. I'm flattered.

JACK. Believe me, Paddy, people began to take me more seriously when I really learned how to talk. It's one of the most evident signs of cultivation. It may sound snobbish, but there it is. The reality of the world around us.

PADDY. And yet you think I'm worthwhile, despite the accent?

JACK. You read the likes of Tennyson. That makes you worthwhile. *(There is a knock)* I'll get that.

>   (JACK *answers the door and finds a middle-aged woman,* MRS. JANIE MOORE, *and her young daughter,* MAUREEN.)

JANIE. Oh. I'm looking for—I mean—I mean is this the room of Edward Moore?

JACK. Edward? Oh, you mean Paddy. Apparently I'm not the only one who shrinks from his given name. Please, come in.

PADDY. Mother! Maureen! *(*PADDY *goes and embraces them both)* What are you doing here?

JANIE. We've decided to stay here for a while.

PADDY. Here? You mean you're in Oxford?

JANIE. With how the war is going—well, we thought it best to see as much of you as possible before—well, you never know what could happen. While in training, before you're shipped out—well, we're here temporarily, at least.

PADDY. Well—yes. All of that. And Maureen! How is the violin?

MAUREEN. We're trying to find a new instructor while we're here. My last one was getting to be a frightful bore, so I'm glad.

JANIE. I think Maureen was getting to the point where she was surpassing her teacher. It was time for a new instructor anyway. *(Motioning to* JACK*)* And is this your roommate?

PADDY. Yes, this is my new friend, Jack—I mean Cli—uh, I mean—now what do I call you in a formal setting?

JACK. Please, still just call me Jack. Please. I'll throttle any man who calls me my given name.

JANIE. A pleasure to meet you, Jack.

PADDY. And Jack, this is my mother, Janie King Askins Moore, and my little sister, Maureen.

MAUREEN. A pleasure.

JACK. As it is to meet you, Maureen.

JANIE. Well, I know it's late—you two must have been getting ready for bed soon. But I just wanted to come over, let you know that we were here. But come over tomorrow, if you'd like. I asked your presiding officer and he said that it was your day off.

PADDY. I would love that.

JANIE. Good. Here, I've written down the address. After your training tomorrow, we'll have a good, hearty meal for you. And, Jack, I expect to see you there, as well.

JACK. Well, I think that would be most agreeable.

JANIE. And bring any of your other fellow cadets that you would like. Our house will be open to any of your friends at anytime.

PADDY. Thank you, Mum.

JANIE. Now, here, give me a kiss.

(PADDY *kisses his family good bye.*)

JACK. It was a pleasure to meet you, Mrs. Moore. I'll be there tomorrow.

JANIE. That's an obligation, then. I promise you won't be disappointed by the food.

MAUREEN. Bye, Jack.

JACK. Nice to meet you, Maureen. (*Exit* JANIE *and* MAUREEN) My, my, Paddy, you have quite an agreeable family!

PADDY. Despite their accents?

JACK. Now, Paddy, I think you have misunderstood me. The English may have learned how to talk, but they have this invincible flippancy that I find highly irritating.

PADDY. I second that. There's not a duller people in all of Europe, than the Anglo-Saxon race.

JACK. When it comes down to it, the Irish are the only people, wouldn't you agree?

PADDY. Most heartily so!

JACK. Then we are in perfect unison. And I think I'm changing my views on the accent, even; I'm finding a nice music to it now.

PADDY. I'm glad to see you're coming my way.

JACK. It sounds especially nice from the women, doesn't it?

PADDY. Most certainly so.

JACK. Your mother seems to be quite the gem, you know.

PADDY. Aye, she is. Mrs. Hospitality. Our house was constantly filled with guests. One of the most giving women I know. She certainly likes to be in control and in close proximity, as you can see, but at least she smothers with kindness.

JACK. I must say, Paddy, I'm frightfully jealous. I lost my mother when I was still a boy.

PADDY. Oh, Jack, that's a tragedy.

JACK. Yes, it was. Certainly. Cancer and all that. *(Changing the subject)* What about you? Did you lose your father?

PADDY. No, the man's heart is still beating, unfortunately.

JACK. But your parents aren't divorced?

PADDY. Separated. The ogre won't give Mother a divorce—has to give her less money that way, ironically. *(Changing the subject)* Your father, he's a good fellow?

JACK. Good enough. He's the one supporting me through school and all. We've had a few rows through our life—he's rather mercurial and such. I like to think I take after my mother—she came from a cooler race.

PADDY. I'm sure that's the case.

JACK. But he certainly wouldn't have treated my mother like your father does your sweet mother. My father adored her. He was crushed when she died. Not quite the same since. I don't think any of us were.

PADDY. Well, how about this, Jack? You can borrow my mother. Sort of adopt her as your own.

JACK. Adopt her?

PADDY. Now, this is not an offer I'd make to any chap off the street. My mother, she's important to me. You don't know her very well right now, but I've never seen her turn away anybody in need, I've never seen her not do good when it is good that is offered her.

JACK. And so now you're offering her to me? My, our intimacy has increased dramatically in a few minutes!

PADDY. You'll find that I size people up quickly, Jack.

JACK. Yes, quickly indeed.

PADDY. Haven't you ever had a mysterious bond with a person, somebody who you immediately knew was important to you?

(A piece of one of Wagner's Nordic operas plays lightly in the background.)

JACK. Well, I still write a friend back in Ireland. Arthur Greeves is his name. Lives by my father. He was a kind of a sickly fellow, or so his family led him to believe. Growing up we didn't see each other much, but one day he invites me over and—well, he was reading this book…

PADDY. Our kind of friendships are usually linked by books, aren't they?

JACK. Well, it's common interests that usually draw most friends together, isn't it? And the book that Arthur was reading was one on Norse Mythology. It was one of my passions, you see.

PADDY. Yes, I can see how mythology would suit you.

JACK. You get plenty of pretentious fellows who will go on all about Hades and Zeus and Achilles and Helen. And as much as I adore the Grecian myths, well, Greek is the popular mythology; it's been the popular mythology since—well, Greece. But Arthur, he understood the cold Northern beauty of Loki and Thor and Odin and Brunhilde. Somehow, just living across from each other, we had grown up never realizing we had the same tastes, the same feelings and yearnings towards those obscure, ancient gods. Well, it was the strongest of friendships in an instant.

(Wagner fades off.)

PADDY. Then let's make our friendship one of those, forged together by Tennyson and poetry in a single blow!

JACK. All right, Paddy, it's forged. By the beauty of poetry!

PADDY. And thus you are adopted within my family. My sister will be your sister, and my mother your mother. You can borrow them at any time.

JACK. All right. And you can borrow my father, if he ever comes into town, that is.

PADDY. Splendid. And we'll make a promise.

JACK. A promise?

PADDY. Yes, a pact. A most solemn vow.

JACK. Now, Paddy…

PADDY. A promise between friends, to be trusted upon. I'm very serious about this, Jack.

JACK. All right. Between friends. What is it?

PADDY. Now we both know the death count out there in the war. They're not trenches out there, they're graves. All of our talk of poetry and mythology and high philosophy—it doesn't matter a pence out there. A machine gun will cut through us as easily as anyone else.

JACK. Yes, if Achilles can fall in war, anyone can. No gods will protect us out there.

PADDY. But if one of us makes it, and the other—well, if the other dies—we'll promise here and now that whoever makes it out alive will take care of the other's family. That our parents won't be left without a son to replace the one they've lost. What do you say, Jack?

JACK. Paddy, I promise to do that with all my heart. A most solemn vow.

PADDY. Good. That means we're brothers now.

JACK. Brothers.

PADDY. Good. *(Awkward pause)* Perhaps, then, we should go to bed.

(PADDY *and* JACK *dress into their nightclothes and, by the end of the scene, are in their beds.)*

JACK. With war and vows and blood brothers to feed our dreams.

PADDY. You're not the praying sort, are you?

JACK. Certainly not.

PADDY. Good. Neither am I. Didn't want to endure that ritual every night with you. Felt too much pain in my life to think that there's any one worth talking to up there.

JACK. It's a nice idea, that. God, I mean. Don't have much against the idea of him; I'm a lover of myths, like I said. I just see him as another one of those—Jesus Christ as much as a Loki or Aphrodite or Allah—nice stories, great insights, but I'll be damned if I ever defend them as true stories.

PADDY. Good night, Jack. I'm glad to have a true friend here.

JACK. Good night, Paddy.

SCENE TWO

JANIE *enters to retrieve a tray of appetizers. She sets them down for a moment and sits. A tiredness overcomes her, tinged by a lifetime of grief. She places her hands upon her temples and closes her eyes. Enter* PADDY. *He looks at his mother, sensing her stress.*

PADDY. Mother, go in there and enjoy yourself. Let me take care of the formalities for a while.

JANIE. The party is for you, Paddy. They're your friends.

PADDY. My friends are your friends.

JANIE. Oh, and I am sure that they just revel in the company of their mate's middle-aged mother's social prowess and witty charm.

PADDY. That is most certainly the case. Why, Jack, well, he seemed absolutely bored with everyone but you.

JANIE. Nonsense, he is the life of the party.

PADDY. Of course that seemed the case to you, because you and he talked so much.

JANIE. He misses his mother, I'm sure.

PADDY. If you only knew.

JANIE. What do you mean?

PADDY. Jack lost his mother when he was eight. Cancer.

JANIE. Oh dear.

PADDY. So he and I—well, we decided to substitute parents. I would lay claim to his father if he could lay claim to my mother.

JANIE. So he's the newly adopted son?

PADDY. Especially in case of—well…

JANIE. In case of what?

(Although JANIE *and* PADDY *are unaware of it, the voices in the next room have died down, farewells having been made. Enter* JACK *with* MAUREEN *in his arms,* MAUREEN *giggling loudly.* JACK *is bent over like a hunchback, à la Quasimodo.)*

JACK. Sanctuary! Sanctuary!

PADDY. What in the name of—

MAUREEN. *(Still giggling riotously)* Save me, Paddy! Save me!

JACK. Sanctuary! Sanctuary!

JANIE. Well, save her then.

PADDY. What? Have we suddenly become ten years old?

JANIE. Well, if you won't save my fair daughter, I will.

JACK. Sanctu—

JANIE. Stop, fiend!

JACK. I am no fiend! I am a misunderstood monster!

MAUREEN. Yes, Mother, he's tragically misunderstood! Tragically! But save me anyway!

JANIE. Yes, yes, to the rescue!

(JANIE *goes chasing after* JACK *and* MAUREEN.)

JACK. Sanctuary! Sanctuary!

(*Enter* JOHN "DOC" ASKINS *and* OWEN BARFIELD. DOC *is* JANIE'*s brother, a middle-aged man of a cheery, if not a slightly eccentric, disposition.* OWEN *is a young man of* JACK'*s age.*)

DOC. Paddy, I must say, your friend has amused us to no end!

OWEN. He's as mad as bedlam!

MAUREEN. Precisely! It's wonderful fun!

(JACK *climbs up on the couch,* MAUREEN *still in his arms.*)

PADDY. Oh, Jack, not the couch!

MAUREEN. To Dickens with the couch!

JANIE. Aye! To Dickens with the couch!

(JACK *places* MAUREEN *down on the couch beside him and pantomimes ringing bells.*)

JACK. The bells! The bells!

JANIE. Oh, woe is me, the tragically misunderstood creature has climbed up the bell tower. He is out of my reach! If only some heroically gestured soldier could shoot down the beast and save my poor daughter!

(*They all look to* PADDY.)

PADDY. I think you are all being rather immature.

OWEN. Oh, Paddy, don't be a wet blanket.

PADDY. I am not going to shoot down a classic literary character!

JANIE. Paddy, as your mother, I order you to shoot the tragically misunderstood creature!

PADDY. Oh, all right. *(Without enthusiasm)* Bang.

JACK. Ach! Woe is me! The world has misunderstood me, all because of a hump on my back! And now I am dead!

(JACK *falls to the floor.* MAUREEN *jumps to his side.)*

MAUREEN. Oh! Oh, no! My tragically misunderstood creature is dead! Not even my tears will ever heal him! I die of a broken heart!

(MAUREEN *slumps over* JACK.)

JANIE. Oh! My daughter and the tragically misunderstood creature are dead! I mysteriously die as well!

(JANIE *slumps over* MAUREEN *and* JACK.)

PADDY. Well, then. That solves a good deal of my problems.

(JACK *rises suddenly, casting off* MAUREEN *and* JANIE.)

JACK. By the way, Doc and Owen are the only other guests left. I was supposed to tell you thank you and goodbye.

DOC. He scared the rest of them off when he started doing literary impressions.

OWEN. You should have seen his Man In The Iron Mask. I thought it was brilliant.

DOC. I was rather partial to his Anna Karenina.

PADDY. I'm sure it was lovely.

OWEN. It's been such a lovely night, Mrs. Moore.

JANIE. I'm glad that you enjoyed yourself, Owen. It's been years since I've had such a cultured group—and so young!

DOC. I'll pretend that comment was directed to me as well, Janie.

OWEN. The Doc here outpaced us all! Witticisms abounded!

DOC. And Owen and I found out that we have a good deal in common. I was telling him about my experiences with spiritualism and—

OWEN. Oh, Jack, Paddy, fascinating stuff really—

JACK. You said you were talking about—?

JANIE. Oh, none of that bunk in my house, or I'll turn you all out!

DOC. Well, I have to leave anyway, dear sister. I've got an appointment with a patient early in the morning.

OWEN. I'll go out with you, Doc. We can continue our discussion. A truly capital party, Mrs. Moore.

DOC. And, Janie...take care of yourself, do you hear me? It's not healthy to dwell on the—

JANIE. Yes, yes, I know. If you keep your nose out of all that mumbo jumbo, I'll—

DOC. It's not mumbo jum—

(JANIE *kisses* DOC *on the cheek.*)

JANIE. Take care, big brother. I love you.

DOC. I love you too, Janie. Goodnight, Maureen. Goodnight, Paddy.

PADDY. Goodnight, Uncle.

MAUREEN. Goodnight. Don't forget the sweets you promised!

DOC. I'm a man of my word, sugarplum. Come now, Owen, we're off like phantoms into the night!

(*Exit* DOC *and* OWEN.)

JACK. Phantoms is right, if Doc's talking about what I think he is...

JANIE. Don't give my brother's theories any credence, Jack.

JACK. Believe me, I don't. No ghost stories for me.

PADDY. Here, Maureen, help me clean up in the other room. Let's give Mum a rest—and Jack looks rather tuckered out himself. Climbing Notre Dame and all that.

MAUREEN. That was fun, Jack.

JACK. It certainly was, Maureen.

(*Exit* PADDY *and* MAUREEN.)

JANIE. Well, you certainly liven up the place, Jack.

JACK. Most people consider me a stuffy intellectual.

JANIE. Oh, it seems to me that you have still retained the child in you.

JACK. Funny, that. As a child I always wanted to be a grown-up.

JANIE. Little do children know the troubles that grown-ups have to face.

JACK. I—Paddy told me about your... husband.

JANIE. And he told me about your mother.

JACK. I was just a child when that happened.

JANIE. And thus you got your wish. You had to grow up fast. *(Pause)* You know, I live for moments like tonight. Laughter and light-heartedness and...

JACK. Joy.

JANIE. Joy? I'm not sure how often it goes that far.

JACK. You've been a great hostess, Mrs. Moore.

JANIE. And that's why I do it, isn't it? Surround myself with enough people, enough distractions... It hurts less then, doesn't it, Jack?

JACK. I don't know. Tonight was a bit of a strain for me, actually. Having constantly to be witty and light and... on guard. I prefer a small, intimate group. Two to six people at most. Like we've been at the end here, the four of us and then the two of us.

JANIE. Yes. If the people are agreeable, that is.

JACK. Your family is most certainly agreeable.

JANIE. Joy. You mentioned the word joy. Is that something you feel often, Jack? Are you that at peace with yourself?

JACK. Is anyone truly at peace with himself? No, joy wouldn't be joy if it were my normal state of being. But I must confess, when I use the word it has a unique meaning to me. And it's less euphoric than you would think. There is a... there is an aching involved, a longing.

JANIE. A longing for what?

JACK. For something more. And it is as if this world can't truly hold it for more than a moment. The first time I felt it, I...

JANIE. Yes, Jack. Go on, I'm listening.

JACK. Well, my brother Warren and I spent a good deal of time together as children. We were each other's accomplices in this world. One morning, he brought in this—well, it was a kind of miniature garden he made in a biscuit tin—dirt and leaves and pieces of plants and flowers and little pebbles and the like. I'm sure my sharpened, cynical mind wouldn't think much of it now, but to my child's mind it was as if he had taken Sherwood forest and, with a bit of sorcery, shrunk it down and brought it with all of its magic and wonder to my room. At that moment, I felt something that has been very hard to shake off over the years. It was a mixture of awe and longing and pangs of wind and light reaching into my sinews. It made me feel as if I were a stranger in this world, and I had suddenly caught hold of a glimpse of something else.

JANIE. Of what? Of heaven?

JACK. Well, it would be nice if there were a heaven. If such an idea weren't so attached to that pesky God person, that is.

JANIE. Well, like religion, your kind of joy doesn't go far in making us satisfied with what we have here, does it?

JACK. And I think that's the point.

JANIE. If I didn't know better, I would say that you are in danger of becoming a Christian.

JACK. No, thank you. Better a pagan than a Christian, thank you. If I'm going to force myself to believe in some sort of make-believe nonsense, I would prefer to believe in something a sight more agreeable than Christianity. Perhaps you and I can start a movement back into polytheism. It could catch on.

JANIE. It sounds like a beautiful moment. Your garden in a tin, I mean. I'm sure moments like that don't come often in anybody's life. In fact, I don't think I've ever felt anything quite like that.

JACK. Well, I'm sure you'll get the chance. You have many more years left ahead of you.

JANIE. And is that a good or bad thing?

JACK. Well, Mrs. Moore, whatever I can do to lighten your burdens, I am at your disposal. Consider me—well…

JANIE. A second son.

JACK. Yes.

JANIE. Our home is your home, Jack.

(Enter PADDY *and* MAUREEN.*)*

PADDY. Well, Jack, Maureen's just rattled my ear off about you. I think you've succeeded in supplanting me as the favorite brother.

JACK. That's because you're boring, Paddy.

MAUREEN. That's what *I* said.

PADDY. Traitors, the lot of you.

JANIE. Oh, Jack may be the newest family member, but I didn't give birth to him. You and I have a much deeper bond.

PADDY. Oh, and what is that? Labor pains?

JANIE. I gave you life, yes, through grief and pain and a great deal of yelling and swearing—but you were worth every moment of that, Paddy. You and Maureen both. I'm sure if Jack's blessed mother were around today, she would tell you the same thing about him.

PADDY. Mother, I was only giving Jack some cheek. I wasn't being serious.

JANIE. I was.

MAUREEN. Yes, so serious! Jack, promise me that you'll never be serious like them.

JACK. Serious? Me, what, serious? No, never like them.

MAUREEN. I am glad to hear it.

JANIE. Yes, I think Jack's brand of serious is of a very different sort of species.

(MAUREEN *yawns.*)

JANIE. It looks like it's time for you to be off to bed, Maureen.

MAUREEN. Not likely. I won't be sawing logs while all of you are down here having the fun.

JANIE. Well, that won't happen either, because I think it's time we were all off to bed.

JACK. As much as I would hate to end this delightful evening, I am rather tired myself.

PADDY. We'd better head back, anyway. Don't want them to think we've gone AWOL.

MAUREEN. Do promise that you'll come back, Jack.

JACK. Of course, I will. Haven't you been keeping abreast, Maureen? I am part of the family now.

MAUREEN. A very lovely addition, if you ask me.

PADDY. Look, Jack, she talks about you as if you were the new family dog.

JACK. If that were the only way to gain membership into the family, I would gladly do that, too.

JANIE. Come now, Maureen, it is off to bed with the both of us. *(Kissing* PADDY *on the cheek)* Good night, love. *(Kissing* JACK *on the cheek)* Good night, Jack. You both can see yourselves out?

PADDY. Certainly, Mum.

MAUREEN. 'Night, Paddy. 'Night, Jack.

PADDY. Good night.

JACK. Good night.

(*Exit* JANIE *and* MAUREEN.)

PADDY. Well done. You certainly made a good impression.

JACK. You're a lucky man to have a family like that. I've never felt such warmth in my life.

PADDY. We are not without our problems. You know that.

JACK. Well, yes, that is obvious. But...

PADDY. Yes?

JACK. Well, I had my brother Warnie, of course. Inseparable, the both of us, but my—well, never mind.

PADDY. I am glad you're here, Jack. Especially with the possibilities that lie before us.

JACK. Oh, honestly, Paddy, I think you're a bit obsessed with the possibility that one of us could...

PADDY. Again, I'm just glad you're here.

JACK. It's late. Off we go, shall we?

PADDY. Aye.

(Exit JACK. PADDY *gives one last wistful look before he, too, exits.)*

SCENE THREE

ALBERT LEWIS's *home.* WARREN "WARNIE" LEWIS, JACK's *brother, is reading a book. He reaches for a flask in his pocket and takes an exceptionally long draw from it.* ALBERT LEWIS, JACK's *father, enters.* WARNIE *scrambles to hide the flask, without success.* ALBERT *eyes* WARNIE *severely.* WARNIE *speaks with a definite British accent, while* ALBERT *still has a faint Irish accent.*

WARNIE. You're home early. You're never home early.

ALBERT. I had set aside this day when I thought Jack was going to visit us for his month's leave. I had forgotten until I got there. I was going to take both of you to the zoo.

WARNIE. Well, you seem rather sour for a man who has the day off.

ALBERT. That drink is going to kill you someday.

WARNIE. Since when were you a teetotaler?

ALBERT. You're becoming a drunk, Warnie. Don't think that I haven't noticed.

WARNIE. I am no such thing. I am currently very sober, reading on the French seventeenth century.

ALBERT. While taking a very long draw of hard alcohol.

WARNIE. Just something to enliven my senses. A mere swallow. You know, I would like to write a book someday on the French seventeenth century. Very interesting period.

ALBERT. You're changing the subject.

WARNIE. Of course I am. Have you ever read anything on the subject, Father? The French seventeenth century, I mean.

ALBERT. I'm very tempted to take away all alcohol from the house. To take away your flask. I'll burn you dry.

WARNIE. I'm an adult, Father. I haven't really lived at home since you sent me away to school after Mother's—well, you haven't had control over my life for a very long time.

ALBERT. Perhaps that was my mistake, then.

WARNIE. Perhaps, but what's really bothering you, Father? All agitated because Jack isn't here?

ALBERT. Jack has nothing to do with this conversation.

WARNIE. Jack has everything to do with this conversation.

ALBERT. I repeat myself. Jack has nothing to do—

WARNIE. Jack has a month of leave before he is shipped off from O.T.C. to camp, and half of that leave is already over. He's decided the Moores are more interesting than we are and has opted to stay with them instead of us, and you resent that fact.

ALBERT. This is a rather complicated way of changing the subject—

WARNIE. And instead of trying to build a relationship with your other son, you've brooded over that fact the whole time that I've been here, trying to pretend you're not brooding, which makes you even duller company.

ALBERT. Warnie!

WARNIE. And on this day which you had planned a great deal in advance for, and had hoped for an idyllic, family setting, why, it has fallen flat on its face and you lash out at me on the pretense of your fear that I'll become an alcoholic!

ALBERT. I didn't lash out at you.

WARNIE. You're right. I'm the one who just lashed out at you. But still don't think that I think you care the slightest bit right now about alcoholism.

ALBERT. I—Warnie, even if he doesn't want to be here, does he think that I don't want to see him? He's going off to war! I've supported him in his schooling, I've given him a financial crutch—and this is how he repays me?

WARNIE. You know, I'm sorry I brought the blasted thing up.

ALBERT. Does he write to you about this woman?

WARNIE. Who? Mrs. Moore?

ALBERT. Do you know what their relationship is?

WARNIE. I see you're entertaining the same freakish fancies I am. But you don't think it's likely, do you? She's nearly twice his age. Do you know whether she's an intellectual or not? I really can't see Jack fancying anyone but an intellectual.

ALBERT. Jack's been a good boy that way, hasn't he?

WARNIE. Well, you know that I'm not precisely old fashioned, Father. If she was loose by nature, then I don't think there would be a thing to it. But if she's overly sentimental or some rot like that—well…

ALBERT. It frightens me.

(A door is heard opening in another part of the house.)

JACK. *(Off-stage)* Hello? Is anyone here?

ALBERT. Jack?

WARNIE. Why, the devil did come! Jack, Jack, back here!

(Enter JACK *with his traveling bags.* WARNIE *goes and embraces him, while* ALBERT *hangs back a bit.)*

WARNIE. Why didn't you wire that you were coming?

JACK. I wanted to surprise you.

WARNIE. Color me surprised.

JACK. What? You didn't think that I would go off without the opportunity of seeing both of you?

ALBERT. The thought had crossed our minds.

JACK. Sir.

ALBERT. So you were able to tear yourself away from your precious Moores long enough to drop off for a quick cheerio, were you?

WARNIE. Dad, let's not…

JACK. Aren't you glad to see me?

ALBERT. I would have been glad to see you half a month ago. I would have been glad to see you, if I had known that I were a priority to you, instead of you going about gallivanting with a woman twice your age!

JACK. What?

ALBERT. Well, is that what you were doing? Gallivanting?

JACK. I don't think you quite understand—my friend Paddy invited me. I've written to you about Paddy.

ALBERT. Yes, as you've written to me about Mrs. Moore.

JACK. What are you insinuating? Why, I was invited. You just couldn't have expected me to refuse a—

ALBERT. You certainly could have refused it!

JACK. Well, as always, Dad, you're off on your blasted Irish temper.

ALBERT. You're ashamed of me!

JACK. When I see you like this, yes, I am!

WARNIE. Jack!

JACK. You know as well as I do, Warnie, that he's a hopeless case. As always, the mercurial, emotional Albert Lewis! Can't keep his cool once his adrenaline is up. Well, I don't know why I even came now!

(During the argument, there is a knock at the door, which goes unheard.)

ALBERT. What? You already want to run back to that woman?

JACK. Mrs. Moore has nothing to do with this!

ALBERT. Doesn't she?

WARNIE. Stop it, both of you!

(A knock is heard.)

ALBERT. Now, who is that?

(Enter ARTHUR GREEVES.)

ARTHUR. Hello? I knocked, but I don't think anyone heard me.

JACK. Arthur! What a pleasure!

(JACK goes and embraces ARTHUR.)

ARTHUR. I thought I saw a phantom when I first looked out my window, you strolling up to your house. As soon as I saw you go in, I ran over here. Well, I would have run, if not for, you know, my condition. But I walked briskly!

ALBERT. It's good to see you, Arthur. I'll leave you boys to catch up.

WARNIE. Father, wait—what about the zoo? Now we can go. You got work off and everything.

ALBERT. We're not going to the zoo today, Warnie.

(Exit ALBERT.)

JACK. Just let the old man go, Warnie.

WARNIE. You know that I resent the ol' Padada as much as you do,

Jack, but—well, he had planned—oh, never mind. I'll just go help him cool down a bit so that we can all at least have supper together. It may take me a while, but I'll be back.

(*Exit* WARNIE.)

ARTHUR. Did I miss something? A row with your father?

JACK. What else?

ARTHUR. But I thought you two were getting along better.

JACK. So did I.

ARTHUR. What was it about?

JACK. Arthur, has my father been asking you things? Anything unusual, I mean?

ARTHUR. Well, you know your father...

JACK. Yes, that's why I ask.

ARTHUR. He asked for me to hand over the letters you have written me.

JACK. What?

ARTHUR. He said that since you wouldn't tell him about the details of your life, that he would find other means. He said that he would go to any lengths to protect his son.

JACK. And did you give him the letters?

ARTHUR. Of course not.

JACK. Good. Arthur, I want you to burn any correspondence that we've written the last several months—especially anything that has to do with the Moores. I'll do the same with my end.

ARTHUR. But, Jack, I keep my letters. Well, they're our history.

JACK. I don't want to give my father access to my private thoughts.

ARTHUR. Down the road, you'd regret it.

JACK. Really, Arthur, it's not like anyone's going to be scouring through our papers a hundred years from now, wanting to know the intimate details of our lives.

ARTHUR. Well, what if you became a famous poet or writer as you've dreamed of being?

JACK. Even in that unlikely event, I absolutely detest those who try to interpret an author's works through his personal history. A text should be seen in the context of itself, not through journals or letters or trying to read autobiography on every page.

ARTHUR. You're telling me that you wouldn't want access to Shakespeare's journals? Find out who the Dark Lady was? Find out whether Mark Twain was right and see whether the actor Shakespeare was only a front for an even more mysterious man hiding his real identity?!

JACK. Please, Arthur, enough of the melodrama. Just burn the letters.

ARTHUR. All right, Jack. But just for the past few months.

JACK. And I'll do the same. We'll keep the rest.

ARTHUR. So, Mrs. Moore...

JACK. Yes?

ARTHUR. You've written about your feelings for her. Has anything...?

JACK. Feelings are just that: feelings. Chemicals running through the body, synapses in the mind...

ARTHUR. So it isn't...?

JACK. It doesn't matter. Forget that I ever wrote anything about it.

ARTHUR. That doesn't answer the question.

JACK. Forget that I ever wrote anything about it.

ARTHUR. All right.

JACK. The ol' Padada hasn't asked about my religious habits, has he?

ARTHUR. Oh, Jack, don't tell me he doesn't know about that.

JACK. He still thinks I'm going to church. You mustn't tell him otherwise.

ARTHUR. Jack, I mean really, what is it that you're hiding from?

JACK. It's none of his business, Arthur.

ARTHUR. He's your father!

JACK. My father? Arthur, the last several months I have been with a family that has spent time together, that has shared together and laughed together and cared about each other. I felt more a part of a family there than I ever have here.

ARTHUR. I know he's a bit intrusive, certainly not the easiest person to converse with—

JACK. Not unless you want to talk politics or anti-Catholic sentiment.

ARTHUR. —But he needs you. Can't you see that?

JACK. Arthur, when my mother died, he sent us away to school. To one of the most horrible institutions in England. It would have made the Brontës shudder. He didn't take time to properly investigate it, just wanted us out of his sight—

ARTHUR. He was grieving.

JACK. And we weren't? Two young boys, having just lost their mother, you think we weren't grieving?

ARTHUR. Of course you were.

JACK. He walled himself in. Shut the rest of us out. Don't misunderstand me, Arthur, I understand that, I really do. It was a horrible thing for all of us. But when we needed him most, he shut us out. So don't expect me to go rushing to him when he finally feels that he needs us.

ARTHUR. You need to learn to forgive him, Jack.

JACK. Oh, yes, Father Greeves! What, has this become a confessional, a sermon?

ARTHUR. Whoa, don't lash out at me, Jack. I'm your friend.

JACK. I'm sorry, Arthur. I know you mean well, but do you know how condescending you sound when you go off like that? You Christians, thinking you can heal a man's troubles with a few pretty maxims. Forgiveness is a nice Christian principle, but I'm not a Christian.

ARTHUR. And why not?

JACK. Don't go down that path with me again, Arthur.

ARTHUR. Jack—

JACK. Because if you do, I can outtalk you, I can outthink you, I can outmaneuver you. I can crush all your arguments.

ARTHUR. Maybe it's about more than arguments—

JACK. Don't make me do it, Arthur. I know you love your pretty little beliefs, and I don't want to be the one who crushes them for you.

ARTHUR. You can't break them, Jack.

JACK. Truly? If you want me to try, just say the word.

ARTHUR. I—really, Jack, you're overblowing your rhetorical skills just a bit, don't you think?

JACK. Just say the word, Arthur.

(ARTHUR *looks at* JACK *tensely for a moment, deciding...*)

ARTHUR. I don't want to hear my beliefs blasphemed, thank you very much.

JACK. That's what I thought. You know that I love you as one of my dearest friends, Arthur, but I see you over there in your parents' house, protected like an imaginary invalid—

ARTHUR. My ailment is very real.

JACK. Your real ailment has nothing to do with this trumped-up sickness your parents keep you believing in. You could be as healthy as I am, Arthur, but that's not what I'm really worried about. The real prison you live in, the real illness that you have, exists not in your body, but in your mind. Your beliefs are as secure but as fragile as an egg.

ARTHUR. My beliefs are strong.

JACK. How do you know if you never test them?

ARTHUR. *(Pause)* I have nothing to prove to you, Jack.

JACK. You know, Arthur, what you Christians really need is an advocate. A real, hearty, intellectual strength of an advocate, somebody who can stand up to bullies like me.

ARTHUR. You think we're all simple. We're not all simple.

JACK. I have yet to meet the man who proves that point, Arthur.

ARTHUR. But that doesn't mean that you won't.

JACK. All right, I'll take up that challenge. If your God can show me such a man, a man I can respect for his reasoning and talent, then perhaps there is something to your old fairy tale after all. *(With a mocking attitude)* God, if you're there, send me somebody other than pampered lightweights to try their hand at me! *(Back to* ARTHUR*)* Do you want to try and be that man, Arthur?

ARTHUR. Really, Jack, I think we've both had enough of this. You're being rather offensive and...and I don't want to strain our friendship.

JACK. *(With a laugh)* And thus another heathen goes unconvinced.

ARTHUR. So be it, I suppose. But, really, I've had enough.

JACK. Right, right. You have a frail intellectual constitution; must take care, must always take care—

ARTHUR. Really, Jack, don't make fun. My *real* condition is really quite distressing...

*(*JACK *and* ARTHUR *exit, their conversation fading off.)*

SCENE FOUR

MAUREEN *stands in a hospital room, alone, playing the violin. Enter* WARNIE, *out of breath and in military uniform.* WARNIE *stares in surprise at* MAUREEN. MAUREEN *finally notices* WARNIE *and stops playing for a moment.*

MAUREEN. Hello.

WARNIE. I was told that this was Clive Lewis's room. He's my brother.

MAUREEN. Clive? No, I don't think so. I don't know any Clive.

(MAUREEN *begins the violin again.*)

WARNIE. No, they most definitely told me that this was his room.

(MAUREEN *stops again, annoyed.*)

MAUREEN. And I'm telling you most emphatically that this room does not belong to any Clive. Emphatically is a good word, is it not? I heard Jack use it. I think it means seriously.

WARNIE. Jack?

MAUREEN. Yes. Jack. The one who the room really belongs to.

WARNIE. Where is he?

MAUREEN. Where is who?

WARNIE. My brother.

MAUREEN. I told you, your brother isn't here.

WARNIE. Yes, he is.

MAUREEN. You're a stubborn one, you are.

WARNIE. I'm looking for Jack.

MAUREEN. You said you were looking for Clive.

WARNIE. I am.

MAUREEN. Are you funny in the head? For, if you are, I really can scream quite loudly.

WARNIE. I am not funny in the head. I am just—

MAUREEN. Looking for Clive?

WARNIE. Looking for Jack.

MAUREEN. You most certainly said you were looking for Clive, not Jack.

WARNIE. Clive is Jack.

MAUREEN. What?

WARNIE. That's Jack's name—Clive.

MAUREEN. No, Jack's name is Jack.

WARNIE. Jack is his nickname.

MAUREEN. Jack isn't a nickname for Clive.

WARNIE. It's *his* nickname.

MAUREEN. That's nonsense. Jack's a nickname for John.

WARNIE. Well, in this case it is a nickname for Clive.

MAUREEN. I still think you're funny in the head.

WARNIE. Look, would you want to be called Clive?

MAUREEN. Of course not. I'm a girl. Girls aren't called Clive.

WARNIE. Well, if you were a boy would you want to be called Clive?

MAUREEN. Upon the ridiculous presumption that I were a boy—which I'm most emphatically not—I would only want to be called Jack if my name were John.

WARNIE. I don't think we're getting anywhere.

MAUREEN. If I were called Clive, I would not want to be called Jack because then people would think that my name was John and John's a boy's name and I'm a girl. My name's Maureen.

WARNIE. Maureen? Maureen Moore? Jack has mentioned you and your mother in his letters.

MAUREEN. But you don't know Jack.

WARNIE. I do know Jack. Jack is my brother.

MAUREEN. You said that Clive is your brother.

WARNIE. Jack is Clive.

MAUREEN. Is Clive's middle name Jack?

WARNIE. No, it's Staples.

MAUREEN. Staples? Well, that's not a very good name either.

WARNIE. That's why he goes by Jack.

MAUREEN. But Jack isn't a nickname for Staples, either. Jack is a nickname for John.

WARNIE. Look, when he was a little boy, he hated the name Clive and he hated the name Staples, so one day he announced that he was going to be called Jacksie. So we've called him Jack ever since! There's no rhyme or reason to it—that's just what he wants to be called.

MAUREEN. *(Pause)* All right.

(MAUREEN *goes back to playing the violin.*)

WARNIE. Uh, pardon me again—

(MAUREEN *stops again, doubly annoyed.*)

MAUREEN. What is it now?

WARNIE. Where is he?

MAUREEN. Who?

WARNIE. Jack, of course.

MAUREEN. Gone.

WARNIE. Gone? Gone where?

MAUREEN. Just gone.

WARNIE. You don't mean that he's...?

MAUREEN. What? I don't mean that he's what?

WARNIE. Dead?

MAUREEN. Dead?

WARNIE. Yes, dead!

MAUREEN. Are you saying that Jack's dead!

WARNIE. That's what I'm asking you!

MAUREEN. Blessings, no! You had me frightened for a moment. You could scare a girl out of her wits. Jack's as good of a friend as we have.

WARNIE. Now, young lady, I am Jack's brother, and I really want to know where Jack is.

MAUREEN. My mother took him out in the wheelchair, to get him some fresh air.

WARNIE. Wheelchair?

(Enter MAUREEN and JACK, JACK being wheeled in a wheelchair.)

JACK. Warnie, what a surprise!

WARNIE. Jack, you haven't lost the use of your legs, have you?!

JACK. Oh no, nothing so dramatic. The doctors just want me to take it easy. I'm able to take walks alone, when I'm able to convince them.

WARNIE. Bloody hell, Jack, when I got the news, I thought you were here dying!

JACK. Well, as you can see, I'm quite alive.

MAUREEN. Your real name isn't really Clive, is it, Jack?

JACK. Not if I have anything to do with it. How did you get here, Warnie?

WARNIE. I rode fifty miles today, Jack! Fifty miles!

JACK. Fifty miles?! What for?

WARNIE. Because I thought you lay in agony here, dying! In agony! Dying!

JACK. Well, you needn't have done that, Warnie. I only have a some slight wounds. A shell burst near me and I took a few pieces of shrapnel—my sergeant wasn't so lucky, however. I saw him die next to me before crawling back and finding a stretcher. Then they brought me here to Étaples.

WARNIE. But you're all right?

JACK. I actually feel jolly good, besides a good deal of pain in my wrist. The doctor said I should be out of here in a few days.

WARNIE. I borrowed a bicycle, rode fifty miles in one day, and you feel "jolly good?"

JACK. That's the short of it, I'm afraid.

WARNIE. Oh, blast it all, Jack, *I* don't feel jolly good! I'm exhausted! Just a moment ago I was desperate to see you and share with you your last dying breaths, and now I am all sorts of annoyed with you! It really was quite an inconvenience.

JACK. Well, if it helps any, I really am quite touched that you did that for me. I had felt a bit of strain between us lately. But this goes a long way to show how little such things are.

WARNIE. Well, you're out of the war for a bit, aren't you then?

JACK. Yes, thank glory. Warnie—well, I've had a good number of friends die out there. It's been—well, yes, it's been rather frightful.

JANIE. Yes, of the five boys who used to come visit Maureen and me in Oxford, Jack and Paddy are the only ones left. It's been quite a blow for all of us to lose such dear friends.

JACK. Oh, Janie, I've been rude. Warnie, this is my good friend, Mrs. Moore.

WARNIE. Yes, I figured. It's a pleasure, Mrs. Moore.

JANIE. And I see that you've met my daughter, Maureen.

WARNIE. Yes, we've...met. A cracking start.

JACK. Here, Warnie, Janie, will you help me up into my bed?

JANIE. Of course.

WARNIE. Careful now.

(WARNIE *and* JANIE *both assist* JACK *into his hospital bed.*)

JACK. Many thanks.

JANIE. Maureen, perhaps it's best that we give Jack some time with his brother.

MAUREEN. Oh, but I've hardly had a moment with Jack. You've hoarded him to yourself.

JANIE. Jack and I needed to talk. And now Warnie and Jack need to talk.

MAUREEN. Well, what if Jack needs to talk to me?

JACK. Believe me, Maureen, we'll get our chance. And you can play me that piece on the violin you've been practicing. But Warnie has cycled fifty miles in one day—he deserves a few minutes with his invalid brother.

MAUREEN. Well, all right, but only if I can give you a kiss on the cheek.

JANIE. Maureen!

JACK. Well, I feel that I would receive the lion's share from that trade. It's a deal.

(MAUREEN *kisses* JACK *on the cheek.*)

MAUREEN. I hope you get better soon, Jack.

JACK. I'll be out of here in no time.

JANIE. We'll go on a walk. See you in a moment, Jack.

(*Exit* JANIE *and* MAUREEN.)

WARNIE. Well, I see that you still spend a good deal of time with the Moores.

JACK. Yes. They have been good friends.

WARNIE. How good of friends?

JACK. They have been like family to me.

WARNIE. You have a family, Jack.

JACK. Yes, I have you. My best mate, my big brother, my childhood friend who knew me before I knew myself.

WARNIE. You also have a father.

JACK. Yes. That I do.

WARNIE. Does he know about your injury?

JACK. Yes, he knows! Now get off my case about it.

WARNIE. I'm not getting on your case, Jack. But this estrangement that we've both had with him—well, it gnaws on my conscience sometimes…

JACK. As it does to me, Warnie. You think I have no feelings towards him at all? I've written him a good deal this past while. I've pled that he would come and visit. I nearly begged—it takes a good deal to make me beg, you know. I mustered all the lyrical emotion I could—I've written some darn fine, affectionate letters to the ol' Padada, wanting to patch everything, just wanting to see him.

WARNIE. And he hasn't told you that he will come?

JACK. He's not coming. He didn't come right before I was shipped off; he hasn't come since my injury. Janie and Maureen came. You came—you bicycled fifty miles to see me! Yet he can't pry his way out of his daily routine or boot himself from his dusty law cases to see his son who has been wounded in a terrible war, a war I could have just as easily died in. So don't lecture me about the duties of sons until he learns the duties of fathers.

WARNIE. I'm sorry. That is quite the blow that he hasn't come.

JACK. Yes. Quite. I—I've been so depressed. I've lost so many friends—the war is so horrible, a world of craters and without greenery, a world of frozen corpses and half-dead men still moving like crushed insects. And I have these terrible nightmares.

WARNIE. You have them too, eh?

JACK. Well, one nightmare, really. Over and over again. I'd prefer not to say it aloud, lest I jinx it and it haunts me again.

WARNIE. I understand. Well, hm. When I have those kinds of nightmares, I find a good dose of whiskey quiets them soon enough.

JACK. You're not in the bottle again, are you, Warnie?

WARNIE. Now, Jack, if I'm not to lecture you on parental relationships, then you are not to lecture me on drinking habits. Agreed?

JACK. Agreed. They say that you find God in the trenches, Warnie. No, it's not true. All I found was death and blood and senselessness.

WARNIE. Come now, Jack, if you keep broadcasting your Atheism, people will lose confidence in you. God is like any other institution of King or Army or public schools—they're part of a healthy life.

JACK. Whether they be true or not? Is that what religion is to you, Warnie, a mere social institution? God bless king and country and all that rot?

WARNIE. It's just dealing with the outside world. I go along and keep my private thoughts of God, or the lack thereof, to myself.

JACK. Spirit and matter battling. There we are on the battlefield, Warnie, spirits dodging and diving against material bombs and bullets and airplanes, imprisoned in this veil of flesh.

WARNIE. Now you talk of spirits? You sound more like a gnostic now than an atheist.

JACK. There's a spark in us, Warnie. Perhaps, like Wordsworth thought, it has always existed. But if the spirit is truly there, as I feel it is, it is battling against a cruel universe, it is battling a losing war. If I found anyone there on that cratered moon of death and war, it wasn't God, it was the devil. Like Fenris the Wolf trying to swallow the light of the sun.

WARNIE. You've had a hard time of it, haven't you?

JACK. It's been better since I've come here. Why, I had this beautiful little moment the other day. They have this deer park nearby—I was wandering in the bracken, and I came across a stag.

WARNIE. Hm. Quite close, were you?

JACK. Quite close. He was so solemn, had such a steady gaze. There was this...energy to him. There was something—something sacred about him. If there were a God, I would imagine that he would have some of those very powerful, animal-like qualities. The god of nature.

(Enter JANIE, looking absolutely traumatized.)

JANIE. Jack?

JACK. Janie?

JANIE. Jack...

JACK. Where is Maureen?

JANIE. Maureen needs to be alone for a bit—she—we—we've received—a phone call, we received a phone call—well—oh, Jack.

JACK. It's—no, it's—he's not...?

JANIE. The telegram went to my husband first—the wretch hadn't told us, hadn't sent to us—Paddy—oh, my dear, dear Paddy.

JACK. Janie, come here, come here—

(JANIE *goes to* JACK *and embraces him, collapsing and weeping.* JACK *winces slightly from his wounds, but makes no audible sign.* WARNIE, *feeling that he is intruding on a personal moment, exits.*)

JANIE. He's dead, Jack. The War's killed him.

JACK. Shh. Listen, listen here, Janie. This is a terrible blow for all of us, especially for you and Maureen. But know this, please, know this—he saw this. Your boy loved you enough to make sure you would be taken care of. I'm not Paddy, I can't replace him—but I swear to you that I will make sure you and Maureen aren't cast adrift. Woman, behold your son.

(JANIE *looks up at* JACK, *the tears stopping for a moment, and she stares at* JACK *with mingled grief and gratitude.* JANIE *embraces* JACK *again and lights fade to black out.*)

SCENE FIVE

ALBERT *enters, followed by* ARTHUR.

ARTHUR. But Mr. Lewis, you must admit that the book smacks of heresy. It's written on nearly every page.

ALBERT. Why have you come over, Arthur? It was like pulling teeth to get information about Jack from you before.

ARTHUR. I—I'm concerned. He's my friend, and I've been worried about his salvation for a good many years now. This poetry of his, this book—well, I suppose it has opened old wounds.

ALBERT. I'm ecstatic about Jack being published. It's a wonderful success. I won't diminish this great victory in his life.

ARTHUR. Even if it costs him his soul?

ALBERT. Have you seen the reviews yet, Arthur? They're quite complimentary. I've made clippings from *The London Times* and *The Scotsman*, if you want to read them. They've got good eyes; they know that *Spirits in Bondage* is one fine book of poetry.

ARTHUR. You're avoiding my question, sir. All of this academia, this philosophy, this bookishness, this learning of the world—it's dangerous for him. There is nothing more perilous to faith than intellectualism. We're losing him, Mr. Lewis. We've been losing him for a very long time.

ALBERT. Like Jack, you're young, Arthur. He'll soon realize that all of the unfathomable mysteries of the universe can't be solved at the age of twenty.

ARTHUR. He needs our help, sir. He needs our prayers.

ALBERT. Believe me, I've prayed for him every day since he was born. But at some point when you're young or when you're old, you can no longer pretend that the complex ideas of men aren't there. At some point you have to stop running from them. You've got to turn on them, to grapple them and see if you can't get the upper hand.

ARTHUR. But what if a man loses that fight?

ALBERT. God has been with Jack since the beginning. I don't think his experiences haven't been without some tutorial benefit.

ARTHUR. It can't be God's will for a man to lose his faith!

ALBERT. When my wife was dying, Arthur, it was quite the trouble for me. Where was God's reason in that?

ARTHUR. We need to battle against this tide of atheism before it swallows the ones we love. There is reason in death. There is reason in—

ALBERT. Please, let me finish. Flora's death was my crucible. I struggled, and I struggled mightily. I never have quite got over it, but I came out the better man. Faith, when it is pampered, is a weakling, an invalid. But when faith is born of fire and blood and heat and pressure and even doubt—when we are tortured, our flesh scarred with flame, that is when faith is reborn as a stronger, more vigorous being, undaunted against the challenges of a rough existence.

ARTHUR. But Jack's poetry—doesn't it frighten you that he might not come out of that crucible at all?

ALBERT. Honestly, there have been times when I feel that all this education I have been dearly paying for has done more harm than good for my boys. But...but if Oxford doesn't spoil Jack, he may write something that men would not willingly let die.

ARTHUR. Fame? Is that what you're hoping for him?

ALBERT. Not fame, Arthur. I want him to be born into Glory.

ARTHUR. I don't understand, sir.

ALBERT. As I said, my boy, you're still young. Perhaps you'll live to see the day when it comes to pass, and then perhaps you'll understand.

ARTHUR. But, sir—

ALBERT. Isn't it time you went off? Your parents don't like you to strain yourself, do they?

ARTHUR. Well, yes...you know, my condition.

ALBERT. Yes, your condition. You know, Arthur, I have never seen any real evidence of this "condition" of yours.

ARTHUR. I'm a very weak person, Mr. Lewis. I can't strain myself, you see. I have to be careful.

ALBERT. I've been careful for most of my life, Arthur. I'm not sure if it has done me any good. Perhaps if you got out a little more—

ARTHUR. I mustn't put myself in jeopardy, Mr. Lewis!

ALBERT. All right. Well, I'll pray for your health, Arthur, that someday you'll grow strong. I hope someday that you'll be blessed with Jack's strong heart, Arthur.

ARTHUR. I must make do with the one God gave me.

ALBERT. Must you?

ARTHUR. Goodbye, sir.

(*Exit* ARTHUR. *Exit* ALBERT.)

SCENE SIX

JACK's *and the* MOORES' *home. It's midday and a light rain is heard outside.* MAUREEN *is playing the violin, observed by her teacher* MARY "SMUDGE" WIBLIN, *a woman of about* JACK's *age.* JACK *is aside, reading, while* SMUDGE *periodically looks over to him with a rather infatuated look on her face.*

MAUREEN. Is that what you mean, Mary?

SMUDGE. Er, what was that?

MAUREEN. Is it better? Is that the smoother sound you wanted?

SMUDGE. Yes, perfect. You're getting quite good, Maureen.

MAUREEN. Thank you. (*Glancing at* SMUDGE, *who is still looking over at* JACK) Perhaps we should end our lesson early today. You seem a little... distracted.

SMUDGE. Pardon, what was that again?

MAUREEN. Thank you for the lovely lesson.

SMUDGE. Oh, is the time up?

MAUREEN. Perhaps in the future we should have my lessons alone. Next time can you read elsewhere, Jack?

JACK. (*Looking up from his book*) Hm? What was that, Maureen?

MAUREEN. How is it that I can never command anyone else's attention?

Whether poetry or men, something else always seems infinitely more interesting.

JACK. What do you mean?

SMUDGE. What is that you're reading?

JACK. Yeats.

SMUDGE. Do you like his poetry or his closet dramas better?

JACK. Why, Miss Wiblin, do you read Yeats?

SMUDGE. Oh, yes, definitely. And please, I like it better when you call me Smudge.

JACK. Oh, you like our little nickname we christened you with?

SMUDGE. Yes, I like your pet names—nicknames. I meant your, er, nicknames.

JACK. Smudge it is then.

SMUDGE. Well, in the end, Jack, you can call me whatever you darn well please.

JACK. Er—hm—yes.

SMUDGE. *(Nervous)* I'm embarrassing you. I don't mean to embarrass you...

JACK. *(Kindly, trying to ease her nerves)* I knew you were a talented musician, but I didn't know you had a literary turn to you, Smudge.

SMUDGE. Well, yes. I think there is quite a bit you don't know about me, Jack.

JACK. I'm sure that's the case. Perhaps we can—

SMUDGE. Yes!

JACK. Uh, "yes," to what?

SMUDGE. To, er, anything you were about to say. Ha-ha.

JACK. Ha-ha.

SMUDGE. Jack—I don't know why—sometimes when I'm talking to you, I get...

JACK. It's all right, Smudge. You and I have had great conversations. No need to—

SMUDGE. *(Blurting it out)* I think you're one of the finest men I have ever met, Jack!

MAUREEN. Er, Mary, I was thinking about what you said about that Rachmaninov piece, and I think you were absolutely—

SMUDGE. I adore you, Jack!

MAUREEN. *Mary...*

SMUDGE. How do you feel about *me*?

MAUREEN. Mary!

JACK. Er, Smudge, really—what I mean to say is that I've liked our friendship, really, but perhaps this is a little too—

SMUDGE. I'm sorry, Jack, all of that just sort of came out. You know that I am—you know that I'm not...

(Mercifully, JANIE *enters with* DOC *and* OWEN.*)*

JANIE. Truly, John, to think that a grown, educated man like yourself could truly believe in such bunk.

DOC. Well, there's the ol' rationalist talking.

JANIE. Oh, I don't pretend to such intellectual titles as rationalist. Common sense is common for a reason, because it grows out of the obvious. And I think the sort of gibberish you spout off at times utterly betrays your normally stable nature.

JACK. Hello, Barfield. Thank goodness you came in!

OWEN. Good day, Lewis. I thought I'd come out of the rain to visit you, only to step into a bigger storm.

JACK. Well, they are brother and sister after all. Er, Owen Barfield, I don't think you've met Mary Wibelin—we, er, we like to call her Smudge.

OWEN. Hello, Smudge.

JACK. Barfield's a good friend of mine from school.

DOC. Janie, not everything that is true or real can be measured by a ruler or scooted under a microscope. There are other ways of understanding things; there are other senses that can be drawn upon.

JANIE. And there are also delusions, fanciful bogies!

MAUREEN. What's the fuss, Uncle?

DOC. I made the simple suggestion that yoga might help my dear sister's infamous nerves, and then she flies off the handle, listing off my supposed superstitions.

JANIE. Superstitions is putting it lightly. You are absolutely gullible! Thrown about by every fad and supernatural theory! Theosophy. Yoga. Spiritualism. Psychoanalysis.

DOC. Psychoanalysis is a legitimate science!

JANIE. I'm surprised that you haven't invited me to a séance, John.

DOC. Well, I probably would have, if I didn't already know that I would get a tongue lashing for it.

JANIE. You're impossible!

OWEN. So how's your day been, Lewis?

JACK. Very pleasant.

DOC. Well, your narrow-mindedness astounds me, Janie.

JACK. Yours?

OWEN. Besides the weather, I can't complain.

JANIE. I would prefer to be considered narrow-minded than to be taken in by the wings of fancy.

OWEN. Read any good books lately?

DOC. You talk so flippantly about things you have never looked into, never studied, never considered.

JACK. In fact, I was enjoying my reading just now.

JANIE. There are certain things, Robert, that should never be looked into because they are ridiculous from the outset.

OWEN. Really, what are you reading?

DOC. And thus, Janie, you expose your prejudice.

JACK. Yeats.

DOC. *(Breaking from his conversation with* JANIE*)* Yeats? You're reading Yeats?

OWEN. Jolly good, Jack, you broke them from their spell. Now perhaps we can discuss something more civil. Not that I wasn't enjoying the fireworks.

DOC. Not to disappoint you, my boy, but Yeats ties directly into my argument.

JANIE. Yeats is a classic poet, not a supernaturalist.

DOC. O ho! Not to be contrary, dear sister, but, yes, he was.

JACK. I would hate to side against you, Mother, but the Doc's right. In a sense.

JANIE. Oh, don't tell me that you're being taken in by all of this mumbo jumbo too, Jack.

JACK. I wasn't being taken in by anything. I was just trying to get some quiet reading time in, enjoying Maureen's lovely music, and then all hell broke loose.

OWEN. *(Looking out the window)* I think the rain is falling harder.

JACK. But Yeats was a kind of believer in another world, of beings around us, like but unlike us; spirits, fairies, demons, whatever they were, his "ever-living ones" weren't a mere fantasy to him. And there are others—Arthur Conan Doyle, Maeterlinck, probably Shakespeare.

DOC. See, Janie? It's not just chalked up to maniacs and the superstitious. Respectable writers.

JANIE. And this is coming from our resident atheist?

JACK. I didn't say that I gave much credence to it. Not anymore, at least.

OWEN. Well, I do.

DOC. Ah! I knew that Owen would come to my aid! My fellow anthroposophist!

SMUDGE. *(To* MAUREEN*)* He's a what?

MAUREEN. I haven't the foggiest.

OWEN. It's something that I've given a good deal of thought to.

JANIE. The whole world is losing its senses.

OWEN. Now, I'm not talking some sort of magic or dark arts—Madame Bavarsky says that those lead to the kind of supernatural we certainly don't want. Doc's sort of spiritualism may skate a little too close to that sort of thing for my own comfort.

SMUDGE. *(To* MAUREEN*)* Who's Madame Bavarsky?

MAUREEN. Not a clue.

OWEN. But there is something unseen, something spiritual—its really Rudolph Steiner that caught my attention.

JACK. Madame Bavarsky! Rudolph Steiner! I can't believe what I'm hearing. Owen, you're a student of Oxford!

OWEN. I believe what I believe. Steiner and his sort make sense to me.

SMUDGE. *(To* MAUREEN*)* Who's Rudolph Steiner?

MAUREEN. Really, Smudge, how do you expect me to know these things any better than you do?

SMUDGE. Well, you live with them, don't you?

MAUREEN. Well, that's why I took up the violin—so I can drown them out.

(Exit MAUREEN. *Soon her violin is heard faintly from another room.)*

DOC. Well, I personally think that our young Owen here is on the right track—but I may take you aside later and tell you about some of my experiences and see if I can't make you see the sense of Spiritualism.

JACK. But Steiner, Barfield? I mean, he wants to keep the fairy tales of

Christianity while holding on to reincarnation and karma, seasoning it all with his other blasted ideas of the occult and public education—it's a complete menagerie of religions and ideas! You can't have your cake and eat it, too.

OWEN. It's just like you, Lewis, to see with a modern eye, while simply shaking off the ancients.

JACK. It's positively medieval.

OWEN. And what is wrong, even if it were medieval?

JACK. There is a reason why it is called the "dark ages."

OWEN. You assume just because something is not popular or intellectually in fashion that it is not true?

JACK. Well, you know, Barfield, that I am no scientist...

OWEN. Exactly! And yet you take their word because you see them as the most recent authorities. Well, Ptolemy was the authority of his day, and you saw how he played out!

JACK. Yes, another example of a man blighted by the darkness of an unenlightened period.

OWEN. Yes, turn your scrutinizing eye on all other past periods—be the skeptic, be the critic of the mysteries of the past, of the religions of the ancients, of the unseen traditions of great cultures—oh, but by no means turn such an eye on your own "period" or your own intellectual fads or your own flawed ideas. That's a dangerous road, Lewis, for you may find that you are just as "unenlightened" as the so-called Dark Ages of man.

JACK. I think I'm done.

OWEN. You don't like to be challenged, Jack?

JACK. What?

OWEN. You finally meet someone who can stand up to your intellectual bullying, and you just back down?

JACK. I'm not backing down!

JANIE. All right, boys, this may be getting a little heated.

DOC. Why stop them, Janie? After all, you started the fire.

JANIE. And now I'm dousing it. And look, the rain is lifting. Let me walk you home, John. Come now, Mary, and I'll walk you home, too. We'll talk of pleasanter things.

SMUDGE. Oh, but I was hoping that Jack could walk me home.

JACK. Me?

SMUDGE. Well—I thought we could have a nice talk.

JACK. A walk and a talk, eh? Er, hmm, that's sounds nice, but—well.

SMUDGE. We've always had such nice talks, Jack.

JANIE. I suppose that would be quite the nice thing to do, wouldn't it, Jack?

JACK. Yes, under normal circumstances—but Barfield, he just got here! I can't very well abandon him.

JANIE. Very well. You'll have to make do with two middle-aged escorts this evening, Mary.

SMUDGE. Oh, but—

JANIE. Let the boys have their fun, Mary. You must never interfere with a boy's fun. Coming, John?

DOC. I'll be right behind you, Janie. I'll be with you in a moment.

JANIE. All right, but only a moment. Remember you're not as young as you used to be. If you wait too long, you'll never catch up with two vibrant young girls like Smudge and me. Isn't that right, Smudge?

SMUDGE. Oh, but if only Jack could—

JANIE. Right. We're off. Good evening, all.

(*Exit* JANIE *and* SMUDGE.)

DOC. Jack. Owen. Well, I just wanted to say one last thing to you both.

OWEN. Perhaps Mrs. Moore is right, Doc. I'm not sure if we should prolong the conflict.

DOC. No, no, just listen for a moment. Listen for a moment to a man who has been through more life experience than the both of you put together.

JACK. All right.

DOC. Now, I know you both are smart boys, educated boys, but beyond what you learn at school, beyond even what you learned from the wretched experience the war was, there are unseen worlds.

JACK. And the fact that they are unseen doesn't that cast the slightest bit of doubt upon them?

DOC. Let me correct myself: they are unseen by those who do not know where to look—by the uninitiated.

JACK. Oh, and you are initiated?

DOC. Yes.

OWEN. Really, I think this conversation is done. Why don't we—

DOC. I do not talk from book knowledge, or fairy tales, or theories, or mythologies; I talk from rock-hard realities. I talk from personal experience. There is an astral plane upon which we can travel, Jack. There are supernatural beings we can converse with; there are experiences which can tap into the most secret mysteries of the universe.

JACK. You...you say that you have experienced this?

DOC. "We few, we happy few, we band of brothers." You can be part of that brotherhood, Jack.

OWEN. Really, Doc, let's not get him into that sort of—

DOC. That's all I wanted to say. Just think about it. There are ways that you can be initiated into such revelries. There are people who can teach you these things.

JACK. I...I'll think about it, Doc.

DOC. Good. Well, I'd better be off if I'm going to catch the ladies. Goodbye, lads.

OWEN. Goodbye, Dr. Askins.

JACK. Goodbye, Doc.

(Exit DOC.*)*

OWEN. Now, Lewis, you must understand that there is a stark difference between what I advocate and his—

JACK. Is there, Barfield? They sound rather similar to me.

OWEN. There is a darkness around that man, Jack.

JACK. Doc? He's a teddy bear, one of the best friends we have. Always full of kindness and consideration.

OWEN. That's not what I mean.

JACK. I didn't learn anything new today, Barfield. I had a matron at school who was into all of the supernatural theories that both you and Dr. Askins spout off. As a teenager it had a great lure to me. Ironically, the more I studied into the occult, the more I also studied materialism. On one hand, the promise of a spiritual world, and the other, the belief that the physical world was all that there is.

OWEN. You must have had quite the arguments with yourself.

JACK. I swung like a pendulum.

OWEN. And your belief in God?

JACK. God, especially the Christian God, was out of the question.

OWEN. But there is so much in the spiritual history of the world to understand, whether it be through Christianity, Hinduism, Kabbala—

JACK. I will not be taken in again! I've seen through all of that!

OWEN. Calm down, Lewis, I'm your friend. A friendly debate. We've always been able to have a friendly debate.

JACK. I'm sorry, Barfield. You know, if Dr. Askins had made me that offer when I was at the height of my interest in the occult—well, I probably would have become a magician or a wizard of some sort. Literally. But now—well, I'm through with all of that.

OWEN. I sense a hesitancy in your voice.

JACK. I admit—the lure is still there. It sits in me like a dark lust, a vivid interest.

OWEN. Be careful who you take as your guides.

JACK. Even you, Owen?

OWEN. *(With a grin)* Oh, you know that I'm completely trustworthy.

JACK. You stood up to me, Owen.

OWEN. Of course I did. Not going to let *you* win the argument when we know that I'm the better debater.

JACK. *(Laughs)* Hogwash. But, Owen, sometimes... sometimes I think of my experience with Joy. Those times when I have felt that fleeting, but encompassing desire for—for what, Barfield? Could this be it? Another world which I am just not seeing?

OWEN. Why, Jack, are you doubting yourself? Now *that* is a miracle.

JACK. Like I said, you stood up to me. If only more people of your religious bent had that kind of nerve, I might actually develop more respect for religion in general.

OWEN. Perhaps you shouldn't worry so much about how mere humans argue, and instead take the argument to the Great Man Himself.

JACK. I might, if I ever expected a reply.

OWEN. Would you?

JACK. Expect a reply?

OWEN. No, talk to Him. If God came down right behind you tonight and whispered into your ear, what would you say back?

JACK. Don't be so—

OWEN. I'm serious.

JACK. *(Pause)* I'd ask what He did to my Mother.

OWEN. *(Pause)* And what answer would satisfy you?

JACK. No answer, because He doesn't answer, because He doesn't exist.

OWEN. But what if He did?

JACK. Then He's a Coward. Taking mothers from little boys, and giving Mrs. Moore a lousy husband, and letting Paddy get killed in the war, and making His servants into such weaklings, and making my father cold and unfeeling, and never giving any answers... He's a Coward, Owen.

OWEN. What answer would satisfy you, Jack?

JACK. I'm through with this. I'll walk you home.

OWEN. What answer would satisfy you?

JACK. I'm walking you home.

OWEN. *(Pause)* All right. Let's go.

    (Exit JACK *and* OWEN.*)*

END ACT ONE

Act Two

SCENE ONE

We are on Oxford campus. Sounds of the outdoors are heard. HUGO DYSON *is reading in a lounge-like position on the ground, spread out, relaxed, and a little comical.* JACK *enters, stops, gives* HUGO *an odd look, and then is about to proceed when* HUGO *speaks, still not looking up from his book.*

HUGO. Wipe that look off your face.

JACK. Pardon me?

HUGO. That look, it's insulting. Wipe it off.

JACK. What, do you have eyes on the back of your head?

HUGO. Yes, and the top of my head, and the back of my neck, and on my shoulders, thumbs, and big toes. The big toes have the hardest time of it.

JACK. Nothing gets past you, I'm sure.

HUGO. In that you're correct. Nothing gets pass me.

JACK. Except me. Good day to you, sir.

HUGO. *(Finally looking up)* Oh no, you don't!

JACK. Really, I have to go to class.

HUGO. *(Getting to his feet)* There are a lot of "have to"s in this world, and that's not one of them. Believe me, I know—I'm a teacher.

JACK. I find that hard to believe.

HUGO. Believe it or not, it's true.

JACK. Here? At Oxford?

HUGO. Oh, no! Thank the heavens! Who wants to teach at Oxford? I'm a lecturer at Reading.

JACK. But then…?

HUGO. I'm meeting a friend here.

JACK. Well, that's jolly good for you, but I need to go to class.

HUGO. And yet you haven't yet wiped that look off your face.

JACK. And what look is that?

HUGO. Well, it's sort of like this.

 (HUGO *imitates "the look."*)

JACK. Oh, why am I still here?

HUGO. Because nothing gets past me.

JACK. What is your name, again?

HUGO. If I were to reveal to you my real identity, you wouldn't believe me, but mortals call me Hugo Dyson. Pleased to make your acquaintance.

JACK. My name is Jack Lewis.

HUGO. Jack. You don't look like a Jack.

JACK. Oh? And what do I look like?

HUGO. Something more in keeping with the look on your face. Should I call you Chester?

JACK. Jack will do.

HUGO. Well, Jack is rather disappointing, but Jack it is then.

 (*Enter* J. R. R. TOLKIEN.)

HUGO. Ah, here's the friend I was waiting for!

TOLKIEN. Hugo!

HUGO. John! This is Jack Lewis. I wanted to call him Chester, but he would have none of it.

TOLKIEN. It's a pleasure to meet you, Jack.

HUGO. Jack, this is John Tolkien.

TOLKIEN. You're a student here, Jack?

JACK. I'm on my second degree, taking a year's course of English Language and Literature.

TOLKIEN. Ah, good! I'm the professor for Anglo-Saxon literature. Perhaps you can take one of my classes.

JACK. Well, that would be nice, but I won't be taking another term.

TOLKIEN. So you're almost done with school?

JACK. Yes, sir.

TOLKIEN. Oh, do not call me "sir." I can't be more than ten years older than you.

JACK. I'm twenty-eight years old.

TOLKIEN. Yes, so about six years. Even closer. Then, please, just call me John.

JACK. All right, John.

TOLKIEN. What would you like to do once you've finished your second degree?

JACK. Well… There's not much I can do, I suppose, besides teaching, or perhaps editing for some literary company.

TOLKIEN. Do you write?

JACK. Well, yes. I had one of my poetry books published by Heineman.

TOLKIEN. That's quite the accomplishment.

JACK. But it didn't sell well, despite good reviews. Right now I'm working on a long narrative poem. But, really, how many people really make their name as a writer?

HUGO. Well, you wouldn't want to see the sort of things that John comes up with. He showed me this awful thing called the *Silmarillion*. Frightful bore, certainly not publishable. Its mythology is so thick, it's like reading the Bible.

TOLKIEN. That's why I don't let you read my work anymore, Hugo.

HUGO. And that's the kindest gesture of friendship that you've ever extended to me.

JACK. Mythology?

HUGO. Oh, yes, you'll find us both quite old fashioned when it comes to those sorts of things. None of this T.S. Eliot or other such modern rot.

JACK. Well, you'll find me in perfect agreement with your tastes, then.

TOLKIEN. Truly? Well, Hugo, perhaps we've found a soul mate.

HUGO. Be careful, Jack, he might just start spouting off about little men with furry feet.

JACK. About what?

TOLKIEN. Oh, never you mind. Just this little story that's been running in my mind. It's mainly scraps in my head right now.

JACK. I've had similar things. Why, I've had this image in my head since I was sixteen of a faun, with an umbrella and parcels in his hands, standing by a lamp post in the snow. But I don't know what to do with it.

TOLKIEN. Perhaps you should go onto something else. People might make fun of you if you keep down that line of thought.

HUGO. Especially people like me.

TOLKIEN. Yes, he's more mischievous than Puck.

HUGO. Ach, my true identity has come out! Robin Goodfellow, at your service.

TOLKIEN. Hugo's a bit of a Shakespeare scholar, which I keep trying to pry him out of. Bard, indeed! That blasted man set us back a whole—

HUGO. Oh stop it with your intellectual snobbery, Tollers. Would you like to join us for lunch, Jack?

JACK. Oh, but my—

HUGO. Oh, that. Well, I'm sure if worse came to worse, John could write you a note.

TOLKIEN. A *note*?

HUGO. Second thoughts, perhaps you shouldn't hear this part, John.

(HUGO *covers* TOLKIEN's *ears.*)

HUGO. Skip class and come with us, Jack. It'll be jolly good fun.

JACK. Oh, but... well—

HUGO. Don't you see, Jack? Fate has led us to this moment. There are points in our lives when a vital choice is presented, and not even the patron saints of dusty academics can get in the way of the will of the gods. What do you say?

JACK. Sure. All right.

(HUGO *uncovers* TOLKIEN's *ears.*)

HUGO. Well, we've got a party of three, John.

TOLKIEN. Fantastic. *(Pulling out some candy)* Do you want some Turkish Delight?

JACK. I'm not sure if I've ever had any.

HUGO. Oh, you'll discover whole new worlds with us, Jack.

(*Exit* HUGO, TOLKIEN, *and* JACK.)

SCENE TWO

JACK's *and the* MOORES' *home.* JACK, MAUREEN, JANIE, OWEN, DOC, *and* SMUDGE *are all gathered around the breakfast table, eating.*

MAUREEN. My, my, is that friend of yours still asleep?

JANIE. Maureen, it's not polite to—

JACK. No, no, Janie, it is all right. Arthur lives by his own timetable, to be sure.

MAUREEN. In his own world is more like it.

JANIE. Maureen!

(JACK *laughs*.)

JACK. Mother, Maureen is being absolutely kind. I would more say that he has his own private little solar system somewhere.

OWEN. He's a bit of an odd duck, then?

JACK. Well, I don't necessarily blame the poor man. His family is absolutely convinced that he is an invalid. So to protect his "delicate" disposition he doesn't work, he lives with his parents, he has no real responsibilities.

MAUREEN. Thus the ability to just drop everything and announce to us that he will be visiting for a couple of weeks.

JACK. He is quite the good artist, though. And a decent musician.

DOC. So is it one of those charitable friendships then, Jack?

JACK. Oh, heavens no! Arthur has been one of my closest confidantes since I was very young.

OWEN. He likes Norse mythology, you see. There's no surer way to Jack's heart than mythology.

SMUDGE. I could like mythology.

(*Awkward pause.*)

JACK. Well, it's more than that, you see, Smudge. Arthur and I—well, there are those friendships in which it's not as if you chose each other, but as if you were chosen for each other.

DOC. A divinely ordained friendship, you mean?

JACK. No, that's not what I mean.

OWEN. Well, it sounds awfully like what you said.

MAUREEN. Mother, is this going to turn into another debate?

JANIE. Well, I—

JACK. What I said was—

DOC. Was that certain friends were chosen for each other. By whom were they chosen?

JACK. Don't twist my words on me.

MAUREEN. Because if it is going to turn into another debate, then I think I've lost my appetite.

DOC. Chosen by fate? By spirits?

OWEN. By God? You can't have your cake and eat it too, Jack.

(MAUREEN *exits. Soon we hear her violin in the background.*)

JACK. Please, let's not turn this into another conversation on religion or spiritualism. I've had enough of that lately.

OWEN. You're the one who steered the conversation into that direction, Jack.

JACK. I did no such thing.

OWEN. Your talk was sounding an awful lot like predestination.

JACK. All I was saying was that I think that certain relationships, well, they don't seem to happen by accident.

SMUDGE. So then, Jack, do you believe a man can be meant for a woman?

(*Another awkward pause.*)

JACK. Pardon me?

SMUDGE. Written in the stars and all that. That love is some cosmic force, and that once two people are fated for each other, there is nothing stopping it, nothing standing in its way, there is no escape.

JACK. Uh...

SMUDGE. Because I believe it, Jack. I believe it.

(*Enter* ARTHUR, *in his pajamas, followed by* MAUREEN.)

ARTHUR. Good morning, everybody!

JACK. Arthur! Good morning! Perfect timing, my friend!

(ARTHUR *proceeds to sit and put his feet on the table.*)

JACK. Uh...

ARTHUR. I had an awful time trying to sleep last night. You snore so loudly, Jack. Eventually had to put Indian rubber in my ears. So, what's for breakfast?

JANIE. Jack...

JACK. Yes, Minto, I've got a handle on it. Er, Arthur, I know things may be done differently at your home, but here it isn't polite to wear your pajamas to the table and put your feet up on the dining table.

ARTHUR. Oh, a man mustn't be repressed, Jack.

JANIE. Pardon me?

ARTHUR. Following nature, being one's self...

JACK. Oh, don't tell me you've been reading Freud, Arthur!

ARTHUR. Some people have been introducing me to some of his ideas, yes. Aren't you the one who taught me to be open to new ideas, Jack?

JACK. But don't abandon one stray dog just to pick up another.

ARTHUR. I haven't abandoned anything. I'm still a Christian, Jack.

JACK. I didn't mention anything about Christianity. Not interested in the subject.

ARTHUR. Jack, I've decided that even if I'm not the best spokesman, you need to hear the Gospel declared to you.

JACK. Oh, is that why you're here? To be the good little missionary? No, no, I won't have any of that. Let's go back to Freud. I've decided the only thing sensible about that man is what he says about the relationships of children and parents. Carl Jung is the only one from the Viennese school with any true sense.

ARTHUR. Oh, Jack, you have all the prudishness of a Puritan without any of the religion. Well, if it's Freud you want to talk about, so be it. Freud will be passed down through the ages when the rest of us are forgotten.

JANIE. I don't care about Christian missionaries or which psychologists or philosophers will outlast which. I just want Arthur's feet off the table.

ARTHUR. Oh, but Mrs. Moore, the effect that repression has on the subconscious mind—

JANIE. Arthur—

ARTHUR. The Id and all that—

JANIE. Feet off the table. Now.

ARTHUR. Er, yes. Of course.

(ARTHUR *takes his feet off the table.*)

ARTHUR. But, Jack, I was serious. I'm very concerned for the welfare of your soul—

JACK. Please, just leave my soul alone, Arthur!

ARTHUR. You need to be saved!

JACK. Oh, and now you think you're the man to do it?

ARTHUR. I've finally taken up your challenge.

JACK. No, Arthur, I'm not in the mood for your—

OWEN. Jack, he's come all this way, let him speak his piece.

JACK. I haven't tried to turn you two into atheists—then why are you so intent on converting me? Well, I won't be taken in!

JANIE. Jack, dear, it's all right. How about we all just sit down to some breakfast and—

ARTHUR. But don't you see, Mrs. Moore? He needs the grace of Christ. Or are you an atheist, too, Mrs. Moore?

JANIE. My beliefs have nothing to do with this—

ARTHUR. Mr. Lewis was right! You are a bad influence on him!

JACK. My father has no part in this conversation, Arthur.

JANIE. Oh, is that what he says? Well, if he wants to talk to me about it, my door is always open, but as far as I can see, I'm only doing the job he refuses.

ARTHUR. You are not his mother!

DOC. Young man, if you think you want to help Jack, as you say, then I wouldn't—

ARTHUR. Or do you want to be something more?

JANIE. What?

ARTHUR. Is that rumor true as well?

JANIE. What rumor?

ARTHUR. Because if it is, then I think it's absolutely disgusting and you should repent, and—

MAUREEN. Don't you dare talk to my mum that way!

DOC. I must agree, after being such a good hostess to you, my sister deserves—

JANIE. What rumor?!

ARTHUR. That you and Jack are lovers!

JANIE. What?!

(SMUDGE *suddenly stands dramatically.*)

SMUDGE. Oh, oh…

JANIE. Mary, are you all right?

MAUREEN. Oh no, not again…

SMUDGE. I feel light headed—so, so, flushed and cold…

MAUREEN. She's going to faint.

(SMUDGE *faints. Everyone goes to her side, worried.*)

MAUREEN. Oh, don't worry. She did this when we were playing tennis once. Of course, she had been losing.

JANIE. Mary—Mary, are you all right?

SMUDGE. Oh, oh, everything is so fuzzy.

DOC. Well, let's get her to a bed.

SMUDGE. No! Uh, no—no—no—I need to go home. I'll be all right—if Jack takes me.

JACK. Me?

JANIE. Really, I can...

SMUDGE. IT—MUST—BE—JACK.

OWEN. Well, I'm sure Arthur and I can tag along with you then.

SMUDGE. No. Jack and me—alone.

JACK. All right, Smudge, you and me alone, then. Let me help you.

(JACK *helps* SMUDGE *up.*)

SMUDGE. Oh, Jack, you're so strong.

JACK. I'm a teacher in literature at Oxford, Smudge; my idea of strenuous exercise is a brisk walk. Believe me, I'm no Hercules.

SMUDGE. You'll always be a Greek god to me, Jack.

OWEN. Er, good luck, Jack.

(*The lights fade to black on the back set.* SMUDGE *and* JACK *are lit, indicating that they are now walking outside.* SMUDGE *slips her arm through* JACK's. JACK, *extremely uncomfortable, slips her arm back out.*)

SMUDGE. I passed my Latin exam.

JACK. Oh, jolly good for you, Smudge! That's wonderful news.

SMUDGE. I didn't tell anyone there because I didn't want their remarks. Not tonight, at least.

JACK. After that fiasco, I don't blame you.

SMUDGE. Is it true?

JACK. Is what true?

SMUDGE. What Arthur said about you and...

JACK. Don't give any of that any credence. Arthur's a bit mad. A good friend, but a bit mad.

SMUDGE. That's a relief. (*Pause*) It was all due to your coaching. My exams, I mean.

JACK. Well, it's the least I could do for all the help you've given Maureen with her violin.

SMUDGE. I looked forward to each of our study sessions. I yearned for them each week. Did you?

JACK. Uh, well, yes. Of course.

SMUDGE. Whatever I can do in return for what you've done for me, I'll do it. Anything.

JACK. *(Laughs)* Anything, eh? Well then, I may just ask you to murder somebody for me some day.

SMUDGE. I would, if you asked me.

(Awkward pause.)

JACK. Well—er, yes. Pleasant weather today.

SMUDGE. Oh, Jack, I'm the most miserable creature alive!

(SMUDGE *begins to cry.* JACK *just stands there awkwardly, not quite sure what the proper course is.)*

JACK. Oh, Smudge—Mary, really—you've just had wonderful news—you passed your exam which you had been working so hard towards—why, with your degree in music, and now this degree in Latin and Greek, it puts you in a wonderful position to…

SMUDGE. Oh, what does it matter—what does any of it matter?

(SMUDGE *leans into* JACK, *hoping for his embrace.* JACK *just stands there stiffly, not quite sure what to do. He does not offer her the comfort she seeks.)*

SMUDGE. Oh, Jack, do you really find me so repulsive?

JACK. Mary, of course not.

SMUDGE. All right, I know I'm not the most beautiful woman in the world.

JACK. You look fine, Mary.

SMUDGE. Not fine enough, evidently.

JACK. Mary, now you needn't do this…

SMUDGE. No, Jack, I must. I know that my behavior must seem absolutely erratic at times. The truth of it is, Jack, you make me nervous.

It wasn't always so. I used to talk more than gibberish to you—we used to have nice conversations. I remember when you used to call me sensible.

JACK. And I was sincere in that, Mary.

SMUDGE. Don't think I don't notice the past tense in that, Jack.

JACK. You're reading too much into—

SMUDGE. Am I? Well, I've had a lot to deal with, Jack. After my father's death—in debt, no less—well, the younger children looked to me. My teaching in music is the only thing that has kept us afloat. And put on top of that my education—well, it's been a strain. A very big strain.

JACK. I know, Mary. You've been very strong. I admire you so much.

SMUDGE. *(Laughs bitterly)* Admire me? Yes, that's what every woman wants to hear.

JACK. It's all I have to give.

SMUDGE. Do you love me, Jack?

JACK. No.

SMUDGE. My, that was a quick response. Do you think you could ever love me? I could change, I could…

JACK. No. Never.

SMUDGE. I see. But, Jack, I love you so much, I would do anything to—

JACK. Really, Miss Wiblin, this has got to stop right now. Let me make myself perfectly clear: your advancements are not needed, they are not wanted, they are not welcome. You've put me in some very awkward situations, and I would not like to have them repeated.

SMUDGE. *(Holding back tears)* All right, Jack. That's enough even for my thick head. Goodbye, then.

JACK. Oh—here, Smudge, let me walk you the rest of the way home, at least.

SMUDGE. No, I don't think I would like that—Mr. Lewis.

(*Exit* SMUDGE. JACK *re-enters into his and the* MOORES' *home.* JANIE *is there waiting for him.*)

JANIE. So how did it go?

JACK. Where is everyone?

JANIE. Doc and Owen had to go. Arthur went off to find some nice scenery to paint. Maureen went off with some friends. But you avoided my question.

JACK. What question was that?

JANIE. It was that bad?

JACK. It was miserable, Minto.

JANIE. Did you…?

JACK. I told her the straight truth. I left her no room for misinterpretation.

JANIE. Oh, don't tell me that you were cruel to the poor girl.

JACK. She left me no other choice.

JANIE. There's always a choice.

JACK. I didn't want her to be left with any false hopes.

JANIE. Without leaving her any common kindness to heal the wounds.

JACK. Why are you taking her side on this?

JANIE. You know what that girl has been through.

JACK. Yes, but just because a person's had a rough time of it, it doesn't mean that she can ask for special treatment from others.

JANIE. Why not? Why can't she have "special treatment" from her friends? Why can't she find a place of refuge under this roof, among those of this household?

JACK. I think you're getting a little too worked up about this, Janie.

JANIE. Jack, if there's anything I've tried to create with this home, it is a sanctuary from the toils out there in that vicious society. Both of us have had enough grief in our lives to know how valuable such a place is.

JACK. What would you have me do?

JANIE. Show a little understanding, compassion.

JACK. And let the whole thing go back into its vicious cycle?

JANIE. Do you mean to tell me that you have never been in her shoes? That you haven't loved a person who wasn't attainable to you? That is what you were to her, Jack. And I think, deep down, she knew that her love for you was doomed from the beginning.

JACK. Yes, I think she knew it only too well.

JANIE. And haven't you felt that? That there was someone who, because of circumstance or forces beyond your control, would never be available to you?

JACK. *(Pause)* Yes. I have known that sort of feeling.

JANIE. Then perhaps you can understand why Mary will be crying herself to sleep tonight.

(JANIE *turns to leave.*)

JACK. Minto?

JANIE. Yes, Jack?

JACK. You've had a hard row of it.... How have you not become bitter?

JANIE. Not everything is learned in books, Jack. I can't give you a reading list.

JACK. Do you still feel afraid?

JANIE. Every day of my life. But the time comes when you make yourself utterly vulnerable to the Universe, or Fate, or God, or Science, or whatever controls the strings up there. You say to it, "Inflict upon me your will. I am ready."

JACK. I don't think I could do that.

JANIE. The day may come when you have to.

JACK. Minto... Theoretically speaking of course, if God came to you, what would say to Him?

JANIE. *(Pause)* I would ask Him why he took my Paddy away from me.

JACK. I'm suddenly tired. I think I need a nap.

JANIE. Rest well then, my boy.

JACK. Thank you, Mother.

(*Exit* JACK. *Exit* JANIE.)

SCENE THREE

JACK, HUGO, *and* TOLKIEN *are putting away chairs. They have just finished a group discussion with the "Coalbiters" and are the last ones there.*

HUGO. Of course, as usual, we're the ones left to put up the chairs.

TOLKIEN. What do you mean, Hugo? I'm usually doing it alone. With Jack in the group now, perhaps I'll get a little more consistent help.

JACK. Quite the nice discussion, that.

HUGO. Yes, until John decided to put his two cents in. Or should I say two pounds—and then ten pounds...

TOLKIEN. You think I'm long-winded, then?

HUGO. You get to the end of your sentences and I've already forgotten the beginning.

JACK. I think Tollers' comments were absolutely splendid. He can't help it if some of the less-attentive can't keep up.

HUGO. While you, Jack, are quite the opposite—you could use a little embellishment.

JACK. Too straightforward for you?

HUGO. There is such a thing as artistry in a man's talk.

JACK. While the only thing you seem to be able to comment on, Hugo, is other people's comments.

HUGO. What—why—I—

TOLKIEN. You're speechless, Hugo? Why, a miracle, Jack! You could turn water into wine! Good show!

HUGO. I wasn't speechless. The infantile nature of the comment didn't deserve a response.

TOLKIEN. Look, his face is reddening!

HUGO. While the smugness on both of yours becomes all the more evident.

JACK. Never mind all that—I must just say, I'm very grateful that you both invited me to this group. It's great fun to talk Norse mythology with others who actually know the difference between a Saga and an Edda.

TOLKIEN. Well, you were a natural invite to The Coalbiters, Jack. There are not many who love to read Old Norse.

HUGO. We're, by nature, a rather exclusive society that way, I'm afraid.

TOLKIEN. We've had some talk of starting another group where we can read our works to each other.

HUGO. I've even agreed to endure Tollers' material, so long as he promises not to be offended if I take a nap every once in a while.

TOLKIEN. You should join up with us when we get it started, Jack.

JACK. Sounds splendid. What are you planning on calling it?

TOLKIEN. I haven't an inkling. By the way, I don't think I've properly congratulated you.

JACK. On what?

TOLKIEN. Now, don't play at a false humility. The fellowship, of course. Welcome to the staff of Oxford. You're an educator now.

HUGO. Oh, I don't think I've heard this. Which college are you in?

JACK. I'm teaching English in Magdalen College.

HUGO. Jolly good for you, Jack. I mean that.

JACK. Thank you, both of you. The truth of the matter is that I feel I was one of the least qualified. It stunned me.

TOLKIEN. But it must have been quite the relief.

JACK. Yes, the Moores' and my financial situation has increased a hundred fold by this.

HUGO. Yes, you've been living with that woman and her daughter.

TOLKIEN. Wait—don't tell me that you've been supporting them, Jack.

JACK. Well, yes.

TOLKIEN. On what?

JACK. On a little money I get from serving in the war and on—well, on an allowance that my father sends to support me through school.

TOLKIEN. Yes, to support *you*. Did your father know that it was also supporting two others, one of them with her own school bills to pay?

JACK. No.

HUGO. My, my, Jack. You must have made that money go far.

JACK. We survived. We scraped by. But now that's all done.

TOLKIEN. Then this has been a blessing from heaven in more than one way.

JACK. I don't think heaven had much to do with it.

TOLKIEN. Oh, that's right. You're not religious, are you?

JACK. Of course not.

(There is an awkward pause.)

JACK. Wait a minute, you're not saying that *you* are.

TOLKIEN. I suppose it hasn't come up in conversation, has it?

JACK. Blimey! Don't tell me that you're Christians!

HUGO. What's worse, Jack, Tolkien's a Papist. I've tried to make him see the light, but, alas, to no avail. The Reformation will not touch him.

JACK. Tollers—you're a Catholic?

TOLKIEN. Why should that come as such a big surprise to you, Jack?

JACK. How is that all my best friends end up believing in such nonsense? What attracts you blighters to me?

TOLKIEN. Now, Jack, you're bordering on the offensive.

JACK. You're both educated, you're both so intelligent. You teach at Oxford and Reading! You're intellectuals!

TOLKIEN. And you think that all Christians are naturally stupid and gullible, is that it, Jack?

JACK. Well, it's like believing all that we've talked about mythology tonight, well, as if that were all true, too! You should see the earmarks of it—you've been trained in it. There's no difference between Hercules and Jesus Christ!

TOLKIEN. Have some respect!

JACK. You believe in a fairy tale!

TOLKIEN. Let us be clear on one thing, Jack: we may have different belief systems, but it is an understanding between gentlemen that one does not ridicule or demean another's belief in that person's presence. If you insult my Lord again in my hearing, you will receive a tongue lashing as you've never received before in your life. Is that understood?

JACK. Really, John—

TOLKIEN. Is that understood?

JACK. I—I apologize. I was out of line.

TOLKIEN. Well, I'm glad to hear you say it.

HUGO. *(Pause)* Well, that was an awkward moment, wasn't it?

JACK. It's getting late. Sometimes Mrs. Moore stays up for me, to make sure I get in safe.

TOLKIEN. Jack, I hope...

JACK. I'll see you next Wednesday—same time, same place?

TOLKIEN. Yes. Same time, same place.

JACK. I'll look forward to it. Good night, John. Good night, Hugo.

HUGO. Good night.

TOLKIEN. Good night.

(Exit JACK.*)*

TOLKIEN. You don't think I came off a little strong, do you?

HUGO. You were defending your beliefs, Tollers. There's never shame in that.

(Exit TOLKIEN *and* HUGO.*)*

SCENE FOUR

Lights raise to reveal the MOORES' *home, with* JACK *reading aloud from "Turn of the Screw" by Henry James. Listening to him are* ARTHUR, JANIE, MAUREEN, DOC, *and* OWEN.

JACK. "…But he had already jerked straight round, stared, glared again, and seen but the quiet day. With the stroke of the loss I was so proud of he uttered the cry of a creature hurled over an abyss, of catching him in his fall. I caught him, yes, I held him—it may be imagined with what a passion; but at the end of a minute I began to feel what it truly was that I held. We were alone with the quiet day, and his little heart, dispossessed, had stopped."

*(*JACK *closes the book. Strangely affected,* DOC *rises from where he is sitting and goes to a window, staring in the distance. A wind is heard faintly outside.)*

MAUREEN. I think the woman is a nutter.

OWEN. What do you mean?

MAUREEN. All I'm saying is that I wouldn't want a woman like that taking care of my children.

OWEN. But isn't the governess the one who ultimately "saves" the little boy?

MAUREEN. Miles dies—how can that be saving him?

ARTHUR. She saves his soul.

MAUREEN. From ghosts that may not be there.

ARTHUR. Are you suggesting that she makes the spirits up in her head?

MAUREEN. Why not? I can see how Henry James leaves room for that interpretation.

OWEN. But the children see them.

MAUREEN. Because she makes them think they see them.

OWEN. I think that takes it a bit far.

ARTHUR. What do you think, Jack?

JACK. Well, it's a bit like Christina dreams, isn't it?

MAUREEN. Christina dreams?

OWEN. When a person sort of—well, fantasizes that they are in the center of a great drama. To escape the mundane, they imagine themselves in the fantastic.

JACK. Yes. There's a bit of a danger in that, isn't it? It makes us discontent with our own lives.

OWEN. Wait a minute, Lewis. Isn't that what we have been just doing, sitting here listening to you read to us—imagining ourselves in an imaginary world?

JACK. Oh, literature is something very different, Barfield. Much healthier.

OWEN. Really? Why is that?

JACK. You disengage yourself. You see through the eyes of another character, not through an alternate version of yourself.

OWEN. I still see no difference.

JACK. The difference is all in the mind. In literature, the identity is never split—

OWEN. Unless you identify yourself as the character.

MAUREEN. Do I need to get out my violin?

OWEN. No, no, hear me out on this. Lewis, your belief systems are incredibly contradictory. On one hand you celebrate all things imaginary—mythology, literature—and accept it as good and right.

JACK. As it should be.

OWEN. But the moment any of that imagination takes any sort of real, tangible shape, when it actually starts to mean anything concrete in the actual world—such as religion or spirituality—you deem it as impossible. When it starts to interfere with your day-to-day affairs, when it seems as if it could tap you on the shoulder, you absolutely duck and hide.

JACK. Poppycock.

OWEN. No, you have to explain and rationalize it away. Thus the war within Jack Lewis: reason versus imagination, spirit versus intellect.

JACK. You've totally misunderstood me.

OWEN. No, I think I've got you pegged.

ARTHUR. Come, now, both of you. Mrs. Moore what did you think of the story?

JANIE. Honestly, I thought it was a bit absurd.

ARTHUR. *(Awkward pause)* All right. And how about you, Doctor Askins?

(DOC *doesn't reply. By this time, this wind outside has picked up a bit.*)

JANIE. John?

DOC. Hm? What is that?

ARTHUR. How did you like the story? "Turn of the Screw."

DOC. Ah. Well, Henry James, he—well, he was just skimming the surface, wasn't he?

ARTHUR. How so?

DOC. Ghosts, spirits—they are only manifestations of a deeper reality, aren't they?

JANIE. Oh, don't go into that rot again.

DOC. It's not rot!

JACK. Hold on, Doc, calm down—

DOC. None of you knows! Owen is the only one of you who suspects it, but he is still as naive as a child!

JANIE. Shh, dear. Calm yourself. You've been so irritable lately.

ARTHUR. This has been going on for a while?

MAUREEN. Be careful what you say, Arthur. You're not without your own personality quirks.

(*The wind outside continues to get more wild.* DOC *becomes more and more erratic and strange.*)

DOC. Children, the lot of you. The incense of this world has you so drugged that you can't even see the shadows on the wall. You can't see the creatures just waiting to prey upon our souls and feast upon us, if we don't cannibalize each other first! Screwed to the wall, each of us—taped and bound.

JANIE. John, really, is this a way for civilized people to talk—

DOC. Civilized! Madame, I have seen astral planes, I have communed with spirits, I have seen more civilization than you have even dared dream up. You all talk of imagination—you haven't enough imagination to see the world as it really is.

JACK. Now, Doc, this isn't funny. You're scaring Maureen—

DOC. Let her see this! Let us not shield anyone from the mysteries—

JACK. Doc, I must insist—

DOC. I know you...

JACK. Of course you know me. We're friends, close friends. Now let us just forget this whole conversation and—

DOC. I know you well, and you are doing as you should, as we had hoped.

JACK. We?

JACK. Clive Staples Lewis—screwed, taped, and bound.

JACK. Please, Doc, stop it—

DOC. Screwed, taped, and bound!

JACK. Stop it!

DOC. You are the enemy! If it comes to it, we will fight you!

JACK. I am your friend, Doc! Janie, what is wrong with him?

JANIE. We may have to call someone. He's been behaving strangely—he's confused...

DOC. Madame, I have more sight than ever before. I can see far distances, into other realms and worlds.

JANIE. Maureen, get out of here. Go outside.

MAUREEN. There is no way I'm—

JANIE. Do not argue with me! Go outside! Arthur, you go with her. Owen and Jack, you stay here.

(*Exit* ARTHUR *and* MAUREEN.)

OWEN. Has he exhibited this kind of behavior before?

JANIE. Not this badly, but yes. His wife has seen the most of it.

DOC. You talk as if I'm not here.

OWEN. I'm not sure who is here.

JACK. Don't talk nonsense. Doc, we think you're sick. We need to get you to a professional.

DOC. Ha! There is no one who can treat what ails us.

(JANIE *goes in and embraces* DOC, *then smooths his face in a comforting fashion.*)

JANIE. Shhh. Come now, brother. Calm thoughts.

DOC. Sometimes I wonder if immortality would truly be a desirable thing, Janie.

JANIE. You've been stressed. He's been stressed, boys. He told me the other day that he is afraid he has cancer. Doctors—always fearing the worst things for themselves.

DOC. You're a good sister, Janie. Thank you.

JANIE. There. That is done.

DOC. I sometimes have the worst thoughts. As if I want to blaspheme everything—obscene and grotesque—twisted. Been having terrible nightmares.

OWEN. Is there anything we can do for you, Doc?

DOC. Owen, remember this—I was a fool to get involved in any sort of spiritualism.

JANIE. Let that go, John. You're sick, that's all. I can call Doctor Hitchens—he would know what to do.

DOC. Oh, Janie, still not seeing the trees from the forest—they are full of shadows...

JANIE. Enough talk of shadows. The problem is in the mind, dear.

DOC. I'll be damned for sure.

JANIE. Doc, no, listen, listen right now...

DOC. They're scratching, tearing, pulling me down—I'm spiraling...

JANIE. Owen, go get Doctor Hitchins.

OWEN. But what if he—?

JANIE. Go. Now!

(*Exit* OWEN. *The wind has blown up to a fury pitch.*)

DOC. Doctor Hitchins is no expert...

JANIE. He will help you.

DOC. Ach! Lunacy and death is at the doors for me! I'm coming to the fiery gates!

JACK. There will be no hell for you today, Doc. I couldn't find a man who's been kinder or gentler to me. Hold on, listen to my voice. We'll talk about this reasonably....

(DOC *begins to move and grimace in strange ways.* JANIE *and* JACK *try to hold him, calm him, which makes him struggle all the more.*)

DOC. "Adders and serpents, let me breathe a while! Ugly hell, gape not!"

JACK. If it is a spirit that has him, it is a literary one! *Doctor Faustus*!

JANIE. Don't talk about spirits! It's only aggravating him!

DOC. "Come not, Lucifer! I'll burn my books!"

(DOC *has dragged them all to the floor. He breaks free from their grip and starts screaming and shrieking.*)

JANIE. John, John, break free!

DOC. Throwing me about the room, flying me through the air, to smash me against the walls—coming in droves, a pack of them sleeking through the shadows, hiding in the corners!

JACK. Try to hold him down, Janie!

DOC. In my bed, feeding on my fever, like gremlins shifting through the sheets—I can almost see them, darting, dragging, biting at my ankles, tearing at my toes—they've come to claim me—they have the deed.

JANIE. He's too strong!

DOC. Damnation is my nectar now—I am to eat of pomegranates. Hell is flowing up to greet me!

JACK. Doc—Doc, listen to me. Ignore whatever is going on in your head and listen to my voice. Let us reason together, let us talk and—

DOC. They reach for my throat, to take my voice. They clutch at my mind and swallow it. They lay waste and plunder to take possession of it!

JANIE. Fate has abandoned us, Jack! It is inflicting us again!

JACK. Be strong, Janie. Don't break now.

DOC. Blackness inflicts my eyes! I am drowning, the mysteries are swallowing me, digesting me, bringing me to burning…

JANIE. John, what is happening to you?!

DOC. "Ah, Mephistopheles!"

(Blackout.)

SCENE FIVE

A light raises on JACK, *who is in a chair next to his father's bed, reading to him from the Bible. More lights raise to reveal the* LEWIS *home.* ALBERT *is bed-ridden, listening intently to* JACK.

JACK. "The people that walked in darkness have seen a great light: they that dwell in the land of the shadow of death, upon them hath the light shined."

ALBERT. Skip to verse six.

JACK. Certainly. "For unto us a child is born, unto us a son is given: and the government shall be upon his shoulder: and his name shall be called Wonderful, Counselor, The Mighty God, The Everlasting Father, The Prince of Peace."

ALBERT. I like how your voice forms the words. Expressive.

JACK. Anything to please you, Father. How are you feeling?

ALBERT. Do you believe them, Jack?

JACK. Pardon?

ALBERT. The words. Do you believe them?

JACK. It's beautiful poetry. Isaiah has a nice way with words. I... I like it very much.

ALBERT. Jack, thank you for reading to me. With Warnie stationed in Shanghai, I don't know what I would have done without you.

JACK. You were always able to hold up quite independently, Father.

ALBERT. Since my retirement—well, this house feels empty. It's... it's nice to have you here.

JACK. It looks as if you need to shave again. I'll go get your razor and cream and you can just sit back, relax, and I can—

ALBERT. There are things I want to tell you before I die.

JACK. Don't exaggerate your state right now, it'll just give you undue stress. The operation was successful and now you need to heal.

ALBERT. The operation was successful, but I didn't tell you, Jack. They...they found cancer.

JACK. Cancer?

ALBERT. They said I should have a few more years, though. But—

JACK. Then we still have a few more years to make things better. As for the moment, you need a good shave, then I'll make you some dinner and—

ALBERT. Jack—

(Enter ARTHUR with an arrangement of flowers.)

ARTHUR. Here you both are. I'm sorry, I—well, I knocked and—

JACK. Yes, Arthur, we know. You let yourself in.

ARTHUR. My mother sent these for you, Mr. Lewis.

ALBERT. That's very kind of Mrs. Greeves. Put them on the nightstand over there.

ARTHUR. There you go.

ALBERT. Give her my most sincere thanks.

ARTHUR. You are in our prayers, sir.

ALBERT. Then I'm sure I'll have a most speedy recovery, if the Greeveses are praying for me. But as it is, boys, I didn't realize how tired I was. I think I need to sleep a while.

JACK. Yes, Father. We'll...we'll talk later. I'll see you out, Arthur.

(The lights dim on the back part of the stage and ALBERT as JACK and ARTHUR move to the front, indicating a change of rooms.)

ARTHUR. How is he?

JACK. Better than expected.

ARTHUR. You've had a rough time of it—your father, and before that—well, Doctor Askin's heart failure.

JACK. Yes.

ARTHUR. How was the funeral?

JACK. It was very cold. I had to borrow a bowler hat and an overcoat just to have enough black things. And I had an awful earache. Oh, and the wreaths and flowers and what not.... Why should lilies ever be associated with such grisly things?

ARTHUR. It was an awful stretch, there, for you for a while.

JACK. Three weeks he went on like that. They chalked it to war neurasthenia. The psychiatrist said that such cases tie back to fear of one's father during childhood.

ARTHUR. Ah, Freud raises his head once again. I thought you didn't give him much credit?

JACK. If it's true, that makes us both susceptible to neurosis, Arthur, since we both were afraid of our fathers. The psychiatrist said to keep away from deep introspection—we mustn't brood or mope, we must stay away from Christina dreams, from vivid daydreaming or play acting.

ARTHUR. Writing? Reading?

JACK. You know I feel that is different. But our sanity, our mental stability—it hangs by the thinnest of webs. We can't risk it; it is too precious.

ARTHUR. And what of spiritualism?

JACK. The doctor said this was a strictly clinical affair.

ARTHUR. And you believe him?

JACK. I—I don't know. But I assure you, I'm cleared of any interest in it. All of this rot about spirits or astral planes—that leads to the path of raving lunatics writhing on the floor. No. Give me the steady, the hum drum, the day-to-day—that's the path for me.

ARTHUR. Jack, I—I hope that you're not associating all things religious or spiritual—well, with the nightmare you've just experienced.

JACK. The thought has crossed my mind. Overheated imaginations in any discipline seem to lead to burnout.

ARTHUR. Jack, wait, wait. Let us look at another possibility. What if it was due to the spiritualism, due to...to darker influences? Then does that not open the possibility to its opposite?

JACK. This is not the time for a sermon.

ARTHUR. No, maybe it is. Maybe it's the perfect time. Jack, listen. If there are supernatural beings who are dark, does it not mean that there supernatural beings who are light? That these stories of devils and angels throughout mythology and history—that there is a kernel of truth?

JACK. I haven't the energy to have this conversation right now, Arthur.

ARTHUR. All right. But think about it.

JACK. Good night.

ARTHUR. Good night.

> (*Exit* ARTHUR. *The lights go up again on* ALBERT *in bed and* JACK *sits by his side.*)

JACK. Are you awake?

ALBERT. Hmmm... Barely.

JACK. I'll let you sleep.

ALBERT. No, Jack, wait.

JACK. Yes?

ALBERT. Do you think of your mother still?

JACK. Yes. Sometimes.

ALBERT. I miss her, you know. I miss her terribly.

JACK. So do I.

ALBERT. I...I wouldn't mind going back to her. I would like to see her again.

JACK. Now don't talk like that...

ALBERT. If anyone deserved heaven, it was she.

JACK. Father—

ALBERT. When Flora was on her deathbed, she was advising her nurse to marry a good man, a man who loved her and a man who loved God. For some time we went on about the goodness of God, and she turned, and—well, the shining that was in her eyes is quite indescribable. Her eyes melted through me as she said, "What have we done for Him?" I burned with light at that moment, and I swore to myself I would never forget that question. We're ingrates towards God, the lot of us.

JACK. I...Father, thank you for sharing that with me.

ALBERT. Your mother loved you.

JACK. I know.

ALBERT. I love you.

JACK. *(Holding back the emotion)* I—I'm here for you.

ALBERT. That means more to me than I can say.

JACK. Now get some sleep.

ALBERT. Good night, my boy.

(JACK *is about to go, but then turns back around.*)

JACK. I love you, Father.

ALBERT. *(Pause)* I'm so proud of you, Jack. No father could be more proud.

(JACK *nods and exits.*)

SCENE SIX

The LEWIS *home.* WARNIE *enters, in a bit of a rush, carrying luggage.*

WARNIE. Jack? Jack? Jack, where are you?

(Enter JANIE.)

JANIE. Jack's not here.

WARNIE. Mrs. Moore? What are you doing here?

JANIE. Jack needed help with the contents of the house. I volunteered.

WARNIE. Where is he?

JANIE. He had a meeting with Mr. Condlin about the estate. That was a couple of hours ago. He should be back soon.

WARNIE. Well, then.

JANIE. Well, then.

WARNIE. What should I do in the mean time?

JANIE. You could lend me a hand upstairs. Going through the books...

WARNIE. Uh, no, that's not my sort of thing.

JANIE. They are your father's books.

WARNIE. I suppose it is good Jack had you come. You seem good around the house.

JANIE. Oh, and is that all I'm good for?

WARNIE. Oh, don't get me wrong, Mrs. Moore. I know Jack prizes you very highly. I... I just hope you don't take advantage of his kindness.

JANIE. What do you mean by that?

WARNIE. Well, the last time I visited all of you in Oxford, well—he's a busy man and I thought he was doing more than his fair share in house work.

JANIE. We all pitch in to help.

WARNIE. While Jack brings in the money. He needs to be focusing on his teaching.

JANIE. I don't see how our affairs are any of your business, Warren.

WARNIE. And I've never seen how Jack is any of yours.

(Enter JACK.*)*

JACK. Warnie? You finally came!

*(*JACK *embraces* WARNIE.*)*

WARNIE. It took me a bit to get here, but—well, what can I say? Military life has its demands and Hong Kong is quite far away.

JANIE. I'll be upstairs sorting through the books if you need me, Jack.

JACK. If you'll just give me a moment, I'll be right there to help you.

WARNIE. Oh, I'm sure the woman can handle herself for now, Jack. I just got here.

JANIE. Uh, yes, Jack, if you and your brother want to talk, I can certainly "handle myself."

JACK. Just give me several minutes with Warnie and then we'll both be up to help. Won't we, Warnie?

WARNIE. Oh, but…

JACK. Thank you for everything, Janie. I don't know how I would have handled all of this without your help.

JANIE. You're very welcome, Jack.

(Exit JANIE.*)*

WARNIE. Why did you bring her here, Jack?

JACK. As I said, you weren't available, so I needed some help.

WARNIE. Well, yes—like I said—the military lifestyle…

JACK. Father died in September. It's now February.

WARNIE. Hm, well, yes.

JACK. You have more of the business mind than I do. All the letters, the estate, the law papers—it's given me a frightful headache. I could really have used you.

WARNIE. I'm sorry, Jack.

JACK. Well, it's nearly done now.

WARNIE. So… Have you handled it well? Father's death, I mean.

JACK. I... When I left him to prepare for the Michaelmas term, he seemed to be doing well, improving. Two days later I got the telegram. I was glad to have that last stretch with him, at least.

WARNIE. I've thought a lot about him since I heard.

JACK. So have I. Mainly regrets.

WARNIE. Yes. Me, too.

JACK. Everything I hid from him—the way we would talk about him, disregard him, neglect him.... It wasn't fair. Especially after all he did to support us.

WARNIE. I'm glad you were able to be with him.

JACK. And yet those last two days... To die without the company of your family. Alone.

WARNIE. Jack—

JACK. But I have felt him, Warnie.

WARNIE. Felt him?

JACK. He's been with me. In this house.

WARNIE. You mean like—like a ghost? A spirit?

JACK. Something. But as much as my reason fights against the feeling, I just can't shake it. It's...it's his...his presence. Helping me. Protecting me from...temptation.

WARNIE. Temptation? Jack, I have never heard you talk like this.

JACK. Neither have I.

WARNIE. Are you becoming religious?

JACK. Religious? I'm not sure if I truly know what that word means or what it means to other people. But...I'm changing.

WARNIE. Into what?

JACK. I don't know. A Christian? A Jew? A Theosophist? A Hindu? A Muslim? A Pagan? I don't know.

WARNIE. I've been going to Church.

JACK. You, too, eh? I don't like it, really. The music is terrible, the sermons are boring, half of the people are asleep, but...

WARNIE. But?

JACK. I go to show that I've taken a side. Even though I don't know which side that is.

WARNIE. Then what are we waiting for, Jack? It's obvious we've been both been touched by something... something bigger than us. Why don't we take the dive?

JACK. Dive? Yes, that's the word. I feel as if I'm standing atop this large cliff at night and being asked to jump off, head first, into a dark yet strangely peaceful abyss. I don't know how deep it is or what's at the bottom of it. Who does that?

WARNIE. Billions of people from different faiths.

JACK. No, I'm not with a billion people on that cliff, Warnie. It's just me. And a Presence. A Presence whispering for me to jump.

WARNIE. Do you trust the Presence?

JACK. I don't know. I don't even know whether he really is there. He could be my imaginary friend, for all I know.

WARNIE. Well, Jack, if you take that plunge, I'll be right behind you.

JACK. No. No, you won't. As I said, it's just me and the Presence.... Warnie, do you ever long for the days in the wardrobe? When you and I would just sit in there and we would tell each other our stories?

WARNIE. Oh, you were always a much better storyteller than I was. Even as a child, your stories of the imaginary land of Boxen and talking, human-like animals—they held me captive.

JACK. Sometimes I wonder if religion is like that. Perhaps something in line with Freud's wish fulfillment. Imagination games. We enchant ourselves, we create an invisible world that does not exist, but because our imaginations are so vivid, so skilled, they become real to us.

WARNIE. Well, maybe some of them are real.

JACK. But Boxen wasn't real, Warnie. It was a place I made up. Talking frogs who dress up and stand like humans, they're not anywhere to be found. Mammals who go on diplomatic missions and sign peace treaties with India—mere fiction. The day came, Warnie, when we had to step out of that wardrobe and go back to the real world.

WARNIE. Did we? Did we really?

JACK. Yes. We had to go to school and find careers and pay bills and act like the grown-ups we always wanted to become.

WARNIE. Only to wish we were children again.

JACK. Feeling Father's presence, my search for that ever-elusive joy, heaven, immortality, a world beyond this—is that all just as made-up as Boxen? A beautiful dream, nothing else? Or is there really something to it?

WARNIE. Well, Jack, I'll say this: it's about time we asked the questions with the real intent of getting the answers.

JACK. There's a barrier in my mind. I can't get over it. There's something that petrifies me from movement, but it's the first time that I have really wanted to be on the other side of the barrier.

WARNIE. That's a very mature thing for you to admit.

JACK. But I'm still petrified. And until I can unpetrify myself and make this stone skin become flesh, it is probably best that we go help Janie with those books.

WARNIE. Oh, but, Jack—

JACK. Oh, come now, Warnie, I know you have an adverse feeling towards housework, but it really is a far stretch. even for you, to use talking religion as a way out of it. Come on.

(Exit JACK.)

WARNIE. Oh, blast it all.

(Exit WARNIE.)

SCENE SEVEN

JACK *is standing in a surreal environment, perhaps smoky, perhaps strangely lit, but definitely shadowed. He looks about nervously, frightened in an almost child-like way. Slowly a* SHADOWED FIGURE *emerges from the darkness and comes up right behind him, whispering in his ear. Is it his father? Is it God?*

FIGURE. Jack...
JACK. I...I'm afraid.
FIGURE. Jack...
JACK. Oh, God...
FIGURE. Jack.
   (JACK *kneels.*)
JACK. Oh, God. Dear God, help me.
   (Blackout.)

SCENE EIGHT

JACK'S *home.* TOLKIEN *and* HUGO *are finishing up a meal, while* JACK *is heard in the background, cleaning up dishes.*

TOLKIEN. Do you believe what you've heard tonight?
HUGO. Perhaps he's gone mad.
TOLKIEN. If so, it's a madness that I would willingly inflict upon the whole world.
   (Enter JACK.*)*

TOLKIEN. So, Jack, now that you're open to the idea of the Divine, would you be interested in hearing the catechisms?

JACK. Oh, I won't let you take me in a time of weakness, Tolkien.

TOLKIEN. Weakness! Hardly, Jack.

JACK. Weakness, I say; I hardly recognize myself.

HUGO. I'd say I've never seen you stronger.

JACK. You're obligated to say that. You're under the same delusion he is.

HUGO. Not so, I'm a child of the Reformation. But I see your point.

JACK. As I said, a "delusion."

HUGO. A "delusion" you're skating rather close to. I never thought I'd see the day when I would hear Clive Staples Lewis espouse the virtues of Theism!

JACK. Use my proper name again and I'll throttle you, I swear I will.

HUGO. My apologies—Jack. (JACK *takes some dishes and goes to exit*) Why, is this a retreat, Jack?

JACK. It's called hospitality, Hugo. You can grab the remaining dishes and help, if you want.

(TOLKIEN *and* HUGO *take dishes and exit with* JACK *into the kitchen. They are still heard.*)

HUGO. It certainly looks like a retreat to me, old chap.

JACK. I can parry off anything you novices put forward.

HUGO. Novices!

(*Re-enter* JACK, TOLKIEN, *and* HUGO.)

TOLKIEN. Yet that's the thing, isn't it? It's not us that you've had to debate lately, is it?

HUGO. A hit, John! A palpable hit!

TOLKIEN. Come now, Jack, how do you expect us *not* to bring this up when you are so clearly emerging into a spiritual life?

JACK. We've had the best education England has to offer. Are we going to throw away our most sharpened reasoning for—for what? Fairy tales? Myths? Legends?

TOLKIEN. Now, you know it's a good deal more than legends.

JACK. Why have I been drawn to you blasted Christians? My closest associates are Christians, my favorite authors—George MacDonald, Chesterton, Bunyan, George Herbert, Dante—they make sense, apart from their Christianity. My atheistic associates, the non-religious authors—they do nothing for me.

TOLKIEN. You know a tree by its fruit, Jack.

JACK. Don't go quoting that damn Bible of yours to me! You must see that I haven't given a pence about any of that in the past.

TOLKIEN. Yes, but that's in the past tense, isn't it?

JACK. John, Hugo, imagine my dilemma—here I was, a thorough atheist—I fought for it!

TOLKIEN. Why the fight, Jack? What comfort is there in such conclusions?

JACK. But that's it! We ought not to believe in something because it's comforting, but because it's true.

HUGO. And yet, didn't you find some comfort in your atheism, Jack? Wasn't there some wish fulfillment there? Invictus, "captain of your own soul," and all that rot.

TOLKIEN. Admit it, Jack. You're more scared now than you've ever been. Why is that?

JACK. I don't know. *(Pause)* I went on a bus ride the other day. On it, I had this...this voice, this feeling come upon me. I realized that I was holding something back, that I was hiding, protecting myself—I was trying to protect my identity. The possession of my own self, my own being.

TOLKIEN. But how can you protect a thing until you have it? You can't truly show your face until you have a face to show.

JACK. Exactly. A choice was placed before me to either stay in my dark cave, protected from whatever was out there, or to expose myself. I didn't feel coerced or forced—it just sat there, a fork in the road, a decision. The bus could go to one destination or another, but now was the moment to decide.

TOLKIEN. And what did you choose, Jack?

JACK. To take off the armor. To submit to this Presence. I seemed destined to make that choice—yet it felt like the most free choice that I have ever made in my life. I went home and prayed for the first time since I was a child. I felt like a child again, utterly vulnerable. There I was on bended knee, the most reluctant convert in all of England.

TOLKIEN. And what happened then, Jack? What happened after you prayed?

JACK. I'm not sure. It's still happening; it hasn't stopped.

(A solemn silence over takes all three of them.)

TOLKIEN. It's a warm night. How about a walk?

(Exit JACK, HUGO, and TOLKIEN. The set is taken away and they re-enter on a bare stage or gravitate to a different section of the stage. The sounds of evening's nature are heard, including a light wind.)

HUGO. But what's the drama, then? If you believe in God now—

JACK. There's a difference between God and Christianity, Hugo.

HUGO. But does God make sense without Christianity?

JACK. Infinitely more.

HUGO. Why, Jack?

JACK. The three of us...mythology binds us together, it's what we love—I appreciate your religion in that context. But we cannot believe something simply because we love it. I can't believe in your Jesus Christ for the same reason I can't believe in Horus, Ra, Cupid, Psyche, Thor, or Loki.

TOLKIEN. You must admit those gods are made of quite different stuff than the Testaments.

JACK. I see many more similarities than differences, John.

TOLKIEN. Such as?

JACK. Such as the "dying god" myth—you can find it many cultures, from the Egyptian Osiris to the Greek Prometheus. Your Christianity may have many things going for it—originality is not one of them.

(There is a pause as they come to a cliff—set-wise, it doesn't have to be any more complicated than the edge of the stage—and they look over it, contemplating it. The sound of the wind has increased slightly. JACK *looks almost frightened.)*

JACK. I can't tell you how much I would love for something like Christianity to exist, to believe that there is something beyond all of this, another world to enter, further up and further in, something only touched upon by imagination. Why, that would be lovely, it would be magical. But how can you ask any modern man to believe in magic?

TOLKIEN. Has it ever occurred to you that Christianity is the true myth?

JACK. There's no such thing as a true myth—myths are nothing but lies breathed through silver.

HUGO. No. No, I believe there's more to them, to all myths. Perhaps something along the lines of inspired imagination, a pre-existent memory that subsists in all people which comes tumbling out in the form of stories.

JACK. Oh, you sound like a psychologist, full of Jung's archetypes and common consciousness.

HUGO. Maybe there is something to that line of thought.

JACK. The psychologists of our day do not lead to God, Hugo. Do you expect our friend Sigmund to jump on this bandwagon?

TOLKIEN. Oh, stop the banter, Jack! Your eternal soul is on the line.

JACK. You forget, Tollers, it wasn't until recently that I believed in a soul. Even now, I don't know what that word truly means.

TOLKIEN. But you know it means something.

(JACK *again looks down the cliff, his nervous fear returning.*)

JACK. Do I? Do I truly? Or is it yet another beautifully told lie? My supposed conversion—what would the Viennese psychologists say about that?

TOLKIEN. You had an experience with God, Jack. Will you forsake Him now for the petty claptrap of mortal resistance?

(JACK *looks even more intently down the cliff, as if he is seeing himself free fall down it.*)

JACK. I jumped off the cliff, but I'm still falling, John.

HUGO. This whole "dying god" myth—think! Myths are a real, unfocused gleam of divine truth falling on human imagination. Think!

TOLKIEN. Yes, think of it, Jack. It's the great and universal myth, one of a dying God who sacrifices Himself for the good of His people. What does that tell us about what we truly know? What we truly know deep inside, locked within us—our need for redemption?

JACK. It's not that simple.

HUGO. Isn't it? I think it is, as simple as a children's story. Oh, the brilliant C.S. Lewis must be involved in something complex, mustn't he? All of us, our brilliant, education-sharpened minds, our fiery intellects, why, we must struggle like great men! Well, Jack, it really isn't about how great we are.

TOLKIEN. Yes, it's about how great He is. Or rather about how good He is. And how we should become like Him.

JACK. Your Christ?

TOLKIEN. No, *your* Christ. The same one you communed with when you prayed.

JACK. John...

TOLKIEN. Christianity is the true myth to which all other myths were pointing. It is imagination made tangible, it is spirit made flesh!

(The wind has increased to a loud fury. For a moment it appears that JACK *is about to jump off the cliff. Blackout.)*

SCENE NINE

In the darkness, the sounds of the wind change to the sounds of a side car motorcycle. Although we don't see them, we also hear the voices of WARNIE *and* JACK.

JACK. How did I let you convince me to step into this death trap?!

WARNIE. Let the wind blow through you.

JACK. This contraption is annihilating space.

WARNIE. *(Laughs)* I saw the look on your face back there—that was exhilaration. You've exposed yourself to the world at a great speed, Jack! Enjoy it! *(The lights come up to the entrance of Whipsnade Zoo.* JACK *and* WARNIE *enter in goggles, leather jackets and other riding clothes.)* Well, we won't have a great deal of time, but I think once Mrs. Moore and Maureen get here, it will be jolly good fun. They weren't far behind us. It was worth it, you'll see.

JACK. The ride alone was worth it.

WARNIE. I thought you called my side motorcycle a "death trap," that we were "annihilating space."

JACK. I hit the water, Warnie.

WARNIE. Pardon?

JACK. A diver is scared until he hits the water, then it's worth it.

(Enter JANIE *and* MAUREEN.*)*

MAUREEN. You two were both going dangerously fast! We could hardly keep up in the car! It was thrilling!

JANIE. A little reckless, if you ask me.

JACK. Well, reckless or not, here we are in one piece. Whipsnade Zoo. Shall we go in?

MAUREEN. I say we shall!

JACK. Jolly good, then.

(*Exit* JACK, WARNIE, MAUREEN, *and* JANIE. *They re-enter and look at the animals in their various exhibits, which are invisible to the audience. They come to a bear. A bear cry is heard.*)

MAUREEN. Look, mum, the bear's watching us.

WARNIE. The blaggard seems rather interested, doesn't he? Is he there for our amusement, or are we here for his?

JACK. He seems a rather lazy fellow, doesn't he, Warnie? We'll call him "Mr. Bultitude."

(WARNIE *and* JACK *laugh.*)

JANIE. Oh, Jack, stop it with your literary references. Not all of us have read every book in the English language. Nor in Greek, Latin, French, German, or Old Norse.

MAUREEN. Mr. Bultitude is a rather comical, pompous fellow in a book called *Vice Versa*, Mother. He's rather like Jack.

JACK. Maureen! I'm impressed.

MAUREEN. I hope you didn't expect me to be a little girl forever, Jack.

JACK. No, I suppose not. I guess we have all done a lot of growing up. But there's still more to do, I'm sure.

JANIE. My, my, is that my Jack showing a bit of humility?

JACK. I think I had to become a child again to really grow up. Make myself vulnerable to the Universe.

JANIE. (*Smiles*) That sounds familiar.

JACK. I learned it from my mother.

(JANIE *quietly takes* JACK's *hand. This is a meaningful moment for them. There is a pause.*)

JANIE. Your real mother would be very proud of the man you've turned into, Jack.

MAUREEN. All right, as interesting as Mr. Bultitude is, let's go on, shall we?

(MAUREEN *and* JANIE *walk off, chatting and laughing.* JACK *stops in front of the lion exhibit.* WARNIE *is about to exit as well, until he notices* JACK *is not following them.*)

WARNIE. Jack?

JACK. He's magnificent. If God were to be an animal, I think he would be a lion just like that. Powerful, good, but certainly not tame. *(Pause)* Do you remember that little miniature garden you made, Warnie? The one in the tin?

WARNIE. Why, yes. That's a long while ago now.

JACK. I had this feeling—this poignant longing. Like I was a stranger in this world. And that little piece of paradise lost you made—it reminded me of the world we came from. It was joy.

WARNIE. Fleeting thing, joy is.

JACK. I've spent the majority of my life searching for it again, trying to relive that moment. I wanted to turn back time and just bathe in it forever. But I've realized something. It was nothing but a road sign, like the ones we saw on the way here. It was pointing me to something, not the thing itself—it was pointing me to something else.

WARNIE. I don't understand a blasted thing you're saying, Jack.

JACK. That's all right. A lot of things in life are like that, though. Stories we tell that point us to something truer.

WARNIE. I'm still just as lost as I was.

JACK. It's simple. I've merely become a Christian, Warnie.

WARNIE. What? When did this happen?

JACK. Sometime between when we left the house this morning and now.

WARNIE. Baptized and confirmed when I wasn't looking, eh?

JACK. I've found what that longing was leading to.

WARNIE. Blimey, you're serious.

JACK. I'm serious.

WARNIE. How?

JACK. I don't know. It's almost as if we traveled there, found a magical gateway on your motorcycle. And here we are in a place much like Boxen—like Mount Olympus, like the Rainbow Bridge, like Prometheus Bound, like the Egyptian afterlife—but not quite. It's something more real.

WARNIE. Blimey.

JACK. Imagination has been made flesh.

WARNIE. How do you think this will affect your writing? Do you think the modern literary world is ready to accept a practicing Christian?

JACK. I've come to a point where I've realized I can't care about those sort of things. I have a greater weight of glory to attend to.

WARNIE. Good for you.

JACK. I feel like Fenris the wolf—I ran and I caught the sun in my teeth and I swallowed it. I thought I was so clever by taking on the sun, by consuming it. But I was so naive, Warnie. If you try to swallow the sun, it will just burn right through you—it will transform you.

WARNIE. Jack, I...

JACK. Can I have a moment alone, Warnie?

WARNIE. Er, yes. Take all the time you need. But this conversation is not over.

JACK. I know. Thanks, Warnie.

   (*Exit* WARNIE.)

JACK. (*Talking to the Lion*) I know that you're not really God, but you're something much like Him—a messenger of sorts. Perhaps you can send this message to Him for me: just tell Him that I am His.

(A brief moment of silence, then JACK *exits.)*

THE END

AUTHOR'S ACKNOWLEDGEMENTS

With the publication of these two plays of mine, there are a number of people I have to acknowledge, due to their influence and importance in creating these plays both in performed and published forms.

My thanks goes to New Play Project (NPP), who produced both of these plays in the Provo Theatre space, which sadly no longer exists in its former function (although I must say that there is some poetry in the fact that it is now a church). Within NPP there were several who were especially helpful. Adam Stallard, I felt, was my tireless advocate and supporter at NPP (not to mention that he acted in both plays and made a stellar C. S. Lewis, bearing a striking resemblance to him). Dave Dixon was an amazing producer and advocate for *The Fading Flower* (and a terrific Tolkien in *Swallow the Sun*, as well as my niece Rachael Stewart's knight in shining armor during the production). Melissa Leilani Larson was an incredibly helpful and insightful dramaturg for *Swallow the Sun*. Arisael Rivera gave invaluable assistance as a producer and member of the cast of the production of *The Fading Flower*. I am also deeply indebted to James Goldberg and Bianca Dillard-Morrison during that period of NPP's growth. Those two particularly provided so much strong leadership and vision to NPP during that time. Although I have moved on with the new theatre organization I envisioned so many years ago, Zion Theatre Company, New Play Project was an important and vital component in my development as a dramatist. Consider this volume a love letter to all of you.

I would be an ingrate if I failed to mention the beautifully talented and supportive casts and crews that I had for both productions. They are as close to a theatrical family as I have. The intimate bonds we shared during those productions were deep and lasting.

I am very grateful to all those individuals involved in the workshop reading of *The Fading Flower* in the Writers/Dramaturgs/Actors workshop at Brigham Young University. Especially since I was a student at Utah Valley University, it was a particular honor to have my play invited to participate in that process. The input from Eric Samuelsen, Wade Hollingshaus, Liz Lund, Stephanie Cleghorn, and Joseph Reidhead bore particular influence on this script during that process.

As far as getting these plays published by Zarahemla Books, I have a few key people to thank. Without the support of Christopher Bigelow, publisher at Zarahemla Books, obviously no one would be reading this. Aubrey Warner and Darlene Young were superb editors in vetting the text for print. Then Ben Crowder's layout for the book is a work of art. I have met few people who are as tirelessly and unselfishly dedicated to progressing the cause of Mormons arts as Ben is.

Finally, I am deeply indebted to my family, both earthly and Heavenly. In particular, Anne has been my patient and loving companion through many years of hardship and glory (not to mention one of my best critics). My father George Stewart has been particularly supportive, providing a large part of the financing for *Swallow the Sun*—not to mention that, especially for a pragmatic businessman/politician, he's been unusually supportive of the idea of his son as a writer and dramatist. I couldn't have asked for a better family. And, of course, these two plays are endlessly inspired by my deep abiding faith in and love of Jesus Christ and my Heavenly Parents.

www.ingramcontent.com/pod-product-compliance
Lightning Source LLC
Chambersburg PA
CBHW031244290426
44109CB00012B/426